"*Nudges from God* is one of those amazing books that speaks to you from the voices of shared experiences. These uplifting stories about the power of God in our lives give every reader an inspirational message to take with them as they journey along their own life path. Powerful and memorable, *Nudges from God* is a book you'll turn to again and again in times of sorrow and in times of joy."

—Shirley Kawa-Jump, Author of *How to Publish Your Articles: A Complete Guide to Making the Right Publication Say Yes*

Nudges from God

An Anthology of Inspiration

Compiled by
Vanessa K. Mullins

Obadiah Press

607 North Cleveland Street
Merrill, Wisconsin 54452

Nudges from God
Copyright ©2003 Obadiah Press

Published by Obadiah Press

Compiled by Vanessa K. Mullins
Edited by Tina L. Miller

Cover art by Melissa Szymanski
Copyright ©2003 Melissa Szymanski. Used with permission.

Page layout by Tina L. Miller

ISBN: 0-9713266-7-3

Printed and published in the United States of America

Dedication

To Gary, Miranda, Zach, and Hannah

Thank you
for giving me the space
and time to follow my
"Nudges from God."

Table of Contents:

Acknowledgments

I would like to thank my mom, Gloria Cornell. It is because of her encouragement throughout my life that I had enough faith in myself to attempt new ventures. Without her sticking by me through the hard times, as well as the easy ones, I would never have made it this far. Thank you, Mom.

I would also like to acknowledge my dad, James Loftus. Though he passed away when I was still a small child, it was his faith that I carry with me now and that I, in turn, share with my own children. I still remember sitting beside him in church every Sunday morning while I learned about God. Thank you, Daddy.

Without my husband, Gary, *Nudges from God* would not have been possible. He gave me the opportunity to spend the time I needed to compile and complete this book. Thank you, Gary, for not only being my husband, but also my friend.

I need to acknowledge my children, Miranda, Zach, and Hannah. They have given of their time with me and eaten many dinners they made themselves while I was working. More importantly, words can never fully express how much it means to me when they ask about what I'm working on, ask to read what I've written, and share my work with their friends. That itself is the highest form of praise I will ever receive even if I live to be 100. Thank you!

Next, is Helen Polaski—who has been there for me since my writing career began. She has encouraged me in all my writing, helped me when I got stuck, and listened to me when I just needed a friendly ear. She has been my friend. Thanks, Helen.

I also want to acknowledge each of the authors. Because of their unyielding faith, *Nudges from God* has become a beautiful testimony to our Lord. Thank you for sharing your stories with the world.

And finally, Tina Miller, the woman who is publishing my book. Tina has been my editor, my publisher, and my friend. Thank you for making my dream come true. Your guidance has truly been inspiring.

— *Vanessa K. Mullins*

1

The Lord Always Provides

...for your Father knows what you need
before you ask him...

— *Matthew 6:8*

A Gift For You From Jesus

By Tressa M. Clinger
Spokane, Washington, United States

About two years ago, I was going through a very low time in my life. My daughter was two, and my son was five months old. My husband's mother was struggling to survive breast cancer. I had recently gone back to school to earn a degree, and my husband severely injured his back and could no longer work. All of this added together, along with trying to raise two young babies, took a huge toll on our relationship, and we grew apart. The children and I left our apartment and moved in with my parents.

Unfortunately, things took yet another serious turn for the worse, and communication with my husband grew more and more strained. He had turned to drugs to cope with the physical pain of his back—everything from prescription medication and injections from his doctor to street drugs and alcohol. As he also attempted to cope with the loss of his wife and children, in addition to the potential loss of his mother, his self-medication grew worse.

I was no better off, even though I tried to convince myself that I was. I took a job as a waitress on the late night shift while my parents watched the children. Gradually, I began spending an increasing number of nights after work at the bar with co-workers. It wasn't long before I was partying like a wild delinquent without a care in the world. There were even nights when I didn't come home until after the sun came up the next morning. I would be passed out just as my children were waking up, and I would sleep away the entire day that I could have spent with my babies. Looking back, it hurts so badly to realize I will never have those days back again.

As a result of the two paths my husband and I had chosen, there was a lot of pointing fingers and hurling accusations between us. Suddenly, one night turned very ugly, and my husband threatened suicide. We drove around the city while we both cried and worked our way through many dramatic hours before finally being able to leave each other for the night.

I was so very afraid at this point and frustrated beyond reason. I could not understand how things only seemed to get worse. I didn't feel I was strong enough to hold back this ceiling of responsibility that seemed to keep getting lower and lower, to the point of nearly crushing me. I felt like I was suffocating. I thought of other 23-year-old girls, and I envied them for being *girls*.

When I felt the pressure was too much to stand, I first tried to run back home to my parents to take care of me and lighten the load. They couldn't do that for me anymore, although they truly tried. Acting like a child by playing with my co-workers as if I had no responsibilities or cares in the world only made my reality scream louder to be heard. Still, instead of facing the real world, I tried to hide away even deeper.

Panicked by my husband's behavior the night before, I called a crisis hotline, and that evening my children and I moved into a domestic violence shelter.

The shelter had its good points and its bad points. On the positive side, our location was completely confidential, which allowed me to regroup without outside stimulation. I was able to reorganize my priorities and focus on my goals more easily. Counseling was available, along with food, clothes, and assistance with finding employment. Outside of these basic needs, there wasn't enough staff to offer much in terms of day-to-day support. For the first time in nearly a year of separation from my husband, I realized what being a single parent really meant.

Without my parents or my husband, it was amazing how difficult it could be to carry groceries up the stairs with an infant and
a toddler at the same time.

We had to be very creative in getting from place to place,
and we never used our stroller as much as we did in the three
months we lived at the shelter. The other women in the shelter
seemed either old enough to be my own mother or on drugs.
There was no one I could really depend on, and our second night
there was one of the loneliest nights of my life. I felt small,
helpless, and alone in this huge world—a world that seemed
filled with hopeless burdens all perched upon my shoulders.

My son was teething—the poor baby was cutting four
front teeth and two molars all at once. I left my daughter sleeping in our closet-sized room to pace the hallways with my
screaming infant son. I walked back and forth for hours as he
wailed against my shoulder. I had to change my shirt three times,
because he'd soaked me with tears and drool, and I could do
nothing for him but pace around until I finally also began to
sob. I began imagining horrible things, and somehow I managed to convince myself that he wasn't only teething, but I must
have given him food poisoning, because I'd fed him lunch with
eggs from the food bank that had passed the expiration date. At
two o'clock in the morning, I dragged my sleeping daughter out
of bed, put both children into the stroller, and took them to the
emergency room where I hysterically informed the doctors and
nurses that they had to either give my son something or give me
something, because I was falling apart. They gave him juice.

The hospital staff was absolutely wonderful and talked
to me for a long time, convincing me that I had not poisoned my
baby. Finally, I calmed down, mainly because no sooner did we
get to the hospital than my son stopped crying. Ask any parent
who has ever taken a sick child to the doctor—this is typical.
Eventually, we put the kids back into their coats and were sent
on our way. My daughter had slept through the entire episode.
When I reached down to adjust her head in the stroller, I noticed

an envelope under her cheek. I never saw anyone put it there, and nobody seemed to be paying any attention to us. I pulled the envelope out and saw, written in blue ink on the outside, this message:

"A gift for you from Jesus."

Nothing else was written on the envelope. I looked inside and found $50. *Now I could buy food and diapers and tampons!* Where did this money come from? How did it get in my daughter's stroller? Gazing at my beautiful daughter, who hadn't even stirred when the envelope was placed under her cheek, and feeling the heavy softness of my son now asleep against my shoulder, I stood in wonder for several moments. Somehow, someone had given me the help that I so dearly needed. My parents couldn't help me, and my friends couldn't help me, but Jesus gave me a gift when I reached a point of feeling so overwhelmed that asking for help from Him hadn't even crossed my mind.

The next day, my mother invited me to go to church with her. I went. At one point, the pastor asked for anyone who felt they needed guidance on their path through life to come forward and accept Jesus Christ as their Lord and Savior. I went to the front of the church, and everyone prayed for me.

As time went on, I found a position teaching preschool where my children could attend daycare with me. I moved from the shelter into my own apartment. I returned to school myself and finally began to feel as if things were coming together. Yet even as I gained more confidence in myself and satisfaction with my life, things still felt incomplete.

One night, I couldn't sleep because I kept thinking of my husband. He was actually no longer my husband, because I had finalized our divorce two weeks prior to this night. Yet he was constantly on my mind. Early the next morning, I called his mother to check on him. "I haven't seen or heard from him for weeks," she told me. "None of his friends know where he is, either. We don't know if he's dead or alive."

I took my children to daycare; then, on my way to college, without even thinking, I turned the wheel and began to drive up and down familiar streets. I drove for two and a half hours. I didn't know where to look, but I searched desperately for him. Finally, I found him walking down the side of the road, and I pulled over. I ran to him and pushed the hair from his thin cheekbones, and I remember whispering, "I can't believe I found you," and he whispered back, "I can't believe you heard me."

I brought him home and made him dinner. Things were definitely not easy at first, because he was going through withdrawals, and he was terrible to look at. But slowly he grew healthier, and we moved to another city far away.

We had been together for four years before being married for three, and the last year of our marriage we spent separated from each other physically, emotionally, and spiritually. We were in different worlds—in our own personal versions of hell—and the time that passed between me finding the envelope from Jesus to the time when we found each other again was a mere three months.

Now, two years later, we are happy together and have a third child. Neither of us had ever considered ourselves "religious," but we know now that someone with more power than either of us would ever have had a purpose for us, and that purpose involves us being together. We have never been happier in all of our years together. We look back and can see how bad things can get, but now we have the confidence that we are being taken care of and any obstacles can be overcome.

A Winter's Tale

By Michelle Guthrie Pearson
Leaf River, Illinois, United States

It's true. God does work in mysterious ways. Sometimes we laugh and shake our heads and write it off as a strange coincidence. But sometimes God's work is so precise and so bold that we can't deny He had a hand in it. In those cases, it really is not a mystery at all. God works in our lives and very clearly lets us know it.

It was the week before Christmas, and my husband had been laid off from his job as a carpenter just six days before the holiday. It was another blow in a long string of misfortunes. A few months before, we had made the decision that I would be a work-at-home mom so I could spend more time with our young son. We were cutting down on childcare costs, convenience foods, car maintenance, and a myriad of other things that go along with a two-income household, and we had thought we were making the right decision, but we began to question that plan after this latest bad news.

We prayed for God to help us maintain our faith, which seemed to be flagging. We prayed that we could keep up with our basic bills and keep food on the table while we weathered this latest storm that had befallen us. We prayed that nothing would happen that would require insurance, because we had neither auto nor health insurance, having let both lapse because we couldn't afford it.

The transmission on our minivan had gone out just after Thanksgiving. Now it really didn't seem like such a big deal compared to the other problems we were facing. A second vehicle didn't seem like such a necessity now that I was no longer working outside the home, but it was still hard to get used to one vehicle. I often felt unproductive at home when I was used to being able to run errands, grocery shop, or do dozens of other things to help with the family chores. But the car was at the bottom of our list of priorities for the moment.

The estimate to replace the transmission was sitting on the desk—$1,639.29. There was no way we could afford it. We had a 12-year-old car that we'd paid $1,200.00 for that was a fairly decent vehicle. In other words, at least it ran and could get us to town six miles away for groceries, church, school, and errands. So we used the car.

One cold Saturday in February, our son was with one of my older daughters, and we took advantage of the alone time to go grocery shopping. We had promised my husband's mother that we would stop at her house in town to pick up a few things she wanted to give us. We were halfway home when I said, "We forgot to stop at your mom's."

"No problem," said Jeff as he turned the corner of a country road that would take us back toward town. This wasn't a road we normally traveled. It was rough and out of the way, but we were halfway between town and home, and that was the nearest road that would get us back to where we wanted to go.

As we were driving down the road, I suddenly saw a flash of red to my right. At the same time I realized it was a snowmobile, I also realized the driver of the machine wasn't going to stop before crossing the road right in front of our car.

I had just enough time to get out a "Watch it!" to Jeff before the snowmobile and the driver slammed against the side of our car and careened down it.

Normally, collisions between cars and snowmobiles don't end well. Just a week before, in a town near us, a teen had been killed when his snowmobile drove into the path of a truck.

Luckily, this time the snowmobiler didn't have a scratch on him. His sled was a bit the worse for wear, but it was mostly cosmetic. However, the tip of one ski had caught in our door and ripped the metal on our car all the way down the side, opening it on the outside like a sardine can.

The snowmobiler gave us his insurance information and told us to call his agent on Monday. We parted, glad that nobody had been injured, but concerned about making a claim for the car when we had no insurance ourselves. Surely the agent would ask us to file with our insurance company first.

Jeff called the agent on Monday, and we were told to bring our car into their drive-in claims office. We weren't expecting much. The car was old, we'd only paid $1,200.00 for it, and the damage was only cosmetic. We certainly didn't want to put more into it than we'd paid for it. We talked about putting any money we might get into Jeff's old pick-up truck, since there was no way the claim would be enough to cover the $1,639.29 we needed for a new transmission for the van.

When we got to the claims office, the adjuster looked at the damage to our car, talked to us a bit about what happened, and asked us to take a seat while he did his calculations and got our check.

He came back a few moments later, handed us a check, had us sign some paperwork, and we were on our way. I got into the car, and Jeff was sitting there with a stunned look on his face. He handed me the check. I looked down at it, saw the amount, and began to cry.

God put us on that road that day. He put that snowmobiler there. He kept him and us safe during the accident. And He put a check into our hands for $1,639.29.

No longer do I shake my head and laugh off seemingly strange coincidences. Nothing is coincidental when it comes to God's protection, His care, His mercy, and His plan for us.

Psalm 25:1-2 says: *"To you, O Lord, I lift up my soul; in you I trust, O my God. Do not let me be put to shame, nor let my enemies triumph over me."*

The Calling

By LaDonna Meredith
Springdale, Arkansas, United States

A closer look at the "birth" of Obadiah Press...
Obadiah Press started from humble beginnings. In fact, our means and methods are still very humble, but our hearts are in the right place!

I envisioned Obadiah Press many years ago. I longed for a publishing company that was different. And I knew that God was clearly calling me to use my talents for His purpose, not for my own. But with a small child (and one on the way), a full-time job, college classes to finish, and other miscellaneous commitments, my longing was put aside. I was waiting for the "right" time to heed His call...

Soon after the birth of my daughter, Alexandria, in February 2000, I began to feel that familiar tug of the Holy Spirit. I felt overwhelmed by what I knew He was calling me to do, and I was fearful of the road ahead. I sat on my couch, holding my sweet daughter, and said, "No, Lord. I cannot do this. I am running the other way. This is not the right time!" I was ashamed by my defiance but literally felt as if I needed to run—and run far away!

But later that night, I opened my Bible and began reading about Jonah. *Like Jonah, I defied God and ran away*, I thought. I quickly closed my Bible and tried to reason that this was just a strange "coincidence." I was not ready to accept that the Lord was still speaking to me.

I called to my then three-year-old son: "Nikolaus, it's time for bed! Pick out a book to read!"

He complied, climbed into bed, and innocently handed me the book he had chosen—*Jonah and the Big Fish.*

I had to hold back tears as I read him the bedtime story. There was now no doubt that God was reminding me of what it was like to be out of His will. And I certainly was not prepared to be swallowed by whatever form of a whale God would send my way! My thoughts were very clear*: I'm ready to listen now, Lord. Forgive me!*

After everyone was sound asleep, I sat at my computer and said, "But Lord, I don't even have a name for this company. I cannot possibly begin this venture without a name." Prompted by the Lord, I opened my Bible to the book of Obadiah.

Obadiah? What kind of a name is Obadiah, Lord? I read on. Obadiah means "servant or worshiper of the Lord."

Yes, Lord, I am Your servant… and Obadiah is the perfect name…

The next morning I posted a message on an Internet group for writers describing my hopes and dreams for Obadiah Press. The response was amazing! God was already blessing my efforts.

That week I met several people who offered their services to Obadiah Press for free or for half price, and I met many, many writers who are now the "core" staff of Obadiah Press.

I also met a dear friend, Tina L. Miller, who is now the Editor in Chief and co-owner of *Obadiah Magazine*….and my contact with Tina quickly reaffirmed God's hand in Obadiah Press.

Tina and I wrote back and forth via email and spoke on the phone for the first couple of days. Her excitement for this project encouraged me and helped to renew my belief in the awesome power of God! She and I decided to write a "mission statement" for Obadiah Press and emailed the statement simultaneously. To our astonishment, the last 22 words of our mission statements were identical—absolutely identical! I immediately fell to my knees in prayer and in praise.

Thank you, Lord! I praise You! And I pray that I will never forget this AWESOME reminder You have given me. You are faithful to Your promises. Thank You, Lord. Thank You!

Tina, too, was in awe of God's power, and we still find it difficult to believe that He is forming Obadiah Press through two women who have only seen each other face to face on two occasions. But He is true to His word, and He has and is continually blessing our efforts by providing for us.

There have been many times that we didn't know how we could go on running Obadiah Press. The financial costs, at times, have been astronomical. One particular occasion, we were literally on our knees in two different states—Tina in Wisconsin and me in Arkansas—praying for a financial miracle. We trusted God and continued believing that He would provide a way. And He did. We received a check that afternoon for the exact amount needed to pay our obligations. This again affirmed to us that God had great things in store for Obadiah Press and *Obadiah Magazine.*

From that day until today... and for the rest of our days, Tina and I have made a vow to follow every door God opens for Obadiah Press. He has given us the strength to ignore the skeptics so that we may faithfully stay on the path He has created for our lives. And, oh, what an exciting time this has been! God has blessed the Obadiah Press website with thousands and thousands of visitors. And we have received hundreds and hundreds of emails supporting this venture. We can't seem to thank or praise the Lord enough for this opportunity!

Tina and I have decided that we will take this company wherever God leads. We take each day one step at a time, following God's lead. He's nudged us in the right direction for the past two years... and we have no doubt He'll lead us into greater things in years to come.

Little Signs

By Heide AW Kaminski
Tecumseh, Michigan, United States

There are times when God sends us little signs to let us know which way to go—or maybe just to reassure us that everything will be OK. Most of the time these signs are subtle or come in ways we don't expect. Thus, oftentimes, we misinterpret these signs or we don't see them at all...Years later, in retrospect, we might suddenly have an "Ah-ha!" moment and recognize what the sign was. God has given me many such little signs.

Yesterday God sent me a sign once again.

It had been a really, really bad day—from little annoying things like stubbing my toe into a wall, to bigger things like a letter with really bad financial news in the mailbox, and then the crème de la crème: my husband came home from a lawyer's office with a huge bill for a retainer. He was being sued, and even though the lawyer assured him that the case was as good as won and that we would probably get some of the retainer back, at the moment, it was another huge bill, and financial stress is not something I handle easily.

When it comes to finances, I have got to be the biggest worrier on this planet.

To top that off, I feel like I have a double burden—as my better half doesn't worry about money at all. If he sees yet another junk truck at the side of the road ("For a bargain! Just $500.00!"), he buys it. "Because I can fix it up and double, if not triple, the money!" he says. (Of course, he forgets to figure in the rent for his storage place and the parts he has to buy to make that truck drivable...)

If he sees the ATM machine spitting out a $559.68 balance on the printout, he doesn't consider the $557.23 we have in outstanding checks. Oh, no, off to his favorite hunting gear store he goes. Later he wonders why I do not share his excitement over that newly acquired $175.00 fishing rod. ("Look, they even threw in a pack of worms for free!")

On this particular day, my husband came home and started tearing the bedroom apart trying to find some papers he needed for this lawsuit. He was looking for documentation about some side work he had done more than two years ago, and he's not the most organized person around. (His filing system consists of putting everything on top of the filing cabinet. Occasionally the pile falls off and gets shuffled around, thus the paperwork is not in any kind of order.)

Then my kids started in. Two of my children were fighting in the living room. The 12-year-old had been roughhousing with the three-year-old for the past half hour and was now screaming at her little brother because she needed to do her homework and he was not ready to quit. The 15-year-old was upset because she couldn't get the computer connected and, therefore, could not check her email.

Our house looked like a disaster area in the wake of Hurricane Hugo! My kitchen was a mess with dishes from yesterday and today, and I was too tired to cook or do dishes.

I was ready to explode.

"I have got to get out of here!" I announced, and I left to go to the grocery store.

I love going to the grocery store. On the drive there, I blast my favorite radio station. At the store, I get free coffee and cookies, and I usually run into people to chit-chat with. If I don't see anyone I know, I make a friend while waiting in line at the checkout or I strike up a conversation with the cashier. And if none of that works out, there are always those entertaining trashy little magazines to read. They make you feel so smart, because you wonder how many people fall for such stupidity and actually buy them.

Needless to say, it is a small way I can escape from everyday stress for a half hour or so.

This time, on the way there, I cried. "Oh God!" I said, "We are in a real big mess here. You have got to help me. *Please!* And please don't expect me to live on pure faith alone here—You know I'm not that strong. I need a sign, and I mean a real good sign. You know how ignorant I am to Your signs. You have to really hit me over the head with your sign, so I see it and know that everything will be OK!"

As I shopped, my financial situation continued to cloud my mind. I finally finished and went to the checkout.

Now, at my store, if the scanner comes up with the wrong price and you catch it afterwards, the store will give you a multiple of the over-scanned amount as a reward/compensation. Well, guess what? Today I found two overcharges and ended up getting $7.10 back! (And at home I found a third item, so I'll have to go back for that one!)

As I was checking out with my extra money—which by far was not enough to pay the bills, but I was debating about investing it into lottery tickets—guess who walked in?

It was the banker we had talked to a week earlier about refinancing our home—a move that would reduce our payments by $200 per month.

We chatted for a few minutes about the weather and had a polite exchange of "how are you's" and other pleasantries. Then, out of nowhere, he started to assure me that, after a few minor technicalities, our loan should go through just fine. He even followed up with a few suggestions on how to speed up the process.

Now did God hit me over the head with a sign or what?

I went home laughing my head off. "Now, God, those are the kind of signs I am talking about! Why can't they always be this crystal clear?"

When I got home, I felt much more peaceful. The dishes had been done, dinner was simmering on the stove, my little one had calmed down, and the teenagers had gone off into different directions to friends' houses.

We will always have troubles to deal with in this life, but if we put our trust in God to lead us through and pay attention to His little signs, everything will be OK.

Only A Whisper Away

By Tina L. Miller
Merrill, Wisconsin, United States

I was raised in a Christian home and learned to pray at a young age, so I grew up knowing God was always there for me. Whenever I had a big problem or concern, I would take it to Him in prayer.

But somehow or another, I got it into my head that I shouldn't bother Him with the little, trivial things in my life. After all, God was already busy dealing with all the millions of people who had *real* problems—*big* problems. He had sick and dying people, grieving people, and wars in other countries to contend with.

He certainly didn't have time for my petty little grievances, squabbles with my siblings, crushes on boys, and the like. I figured it was pretty much my responsibility to deal with the day-to-day stuff on my own—but if I got in over my head, I could always call on God for reinforcements—kind of like calling in the Calvary. I could always count on Him to help me.

I don't know how long it took me as an adult to finally realize that God can handle *all* my problems—no matter how big or how small—and that He *wants* me to come to Him, even with all the little things. He wants to be involved in *every* area of my life—and He wants to be my very best friend, my confidante.

Just like a dear friend here on earth, He wants me to talk with Him about what's going on in my daily life, and He's *never* too busy for me—no matter how trivial my concerns might seem to me.

Amazingly, and unlike my earthly friends who can't always be available at a moment's notice, God is always there for me—day or night, no matter where I am or what I'm going through—and even with all the people on this earth, He still gives me—and every one of His children—His undivided attention. What a miracle! It's beyond my human comprehension.

Once I discovered God's rightful place in my life, I realized I didn't have to comprehend *how* He does it—it's enough to know He just does. So many times I have struggled with something on my own and then suddenly remembered to ask God for His help, and His answer appeared almost instantaneously.

I remember many times when I have been cross-stitching and dropped my needle on the carpet. Diligently searching on my hands and knees looking for it—afraid to just leave it lest one of my children end up with a needle in their foot—I would finally pause a moment, close my eyes, and remember to ask God to help me find it. Afterward, every time, I would open my eyes, and they would immediately fall upon the needle where it lay on the carpet.

Another time, I was designing a cross-stitch pattern for a sampler. I painstakingly plotted out a design featuring a simple birdhouse and created a border of ivy leaves around the piece. Below the birdhouse, I wanted to stitch a Biblical saying about sparrows.

I knew there were passages in the Bible that mentioned sparrows by name, because our pastor had quoted several in church a few weeks before—and he even sang a song about a sparrow. The problem was, I didn't have a clue where to look to find them.

In the faith I was raised in, we memorized a lot of specific prayers, but we didn't study the Bible as a book or memorize scripture verses like my children do in their school today.

So what book would it be in? Old testament or new testament? I didn't have a clue.

But I took out my Bible anyway, set it on my lap, and clasping my hands on the smooth, dark brown cover, I whispered a quiet prayer. "Lord, You know I'm creating these cross-stitch designs to honor You. And You know I have this bird-house here and these nice little ivy leaves, and I was thinking a scripture passage would make it complete. I'm envisioning something about sparrows. Now I know there are Bible passages about sparrows, but I have no idea where to look. Will You help me?"

A moment later, I opened the Bible, put my finger down on a random page, and began to read. And there on that very same page, I found the following passage:

Even the sparrow has found a home,
and the swallow a nest for herself,
a place near your altar,
O Lord Almighty,
my King and my God.
Blessed are those who dwell in your house;
they are ever praising you.
Psalm 84:3-4

Words cannot adequately express how I felt when my eyes fell upon those words—so quickly, so miraculously. To open my Bible—a book of 1,208 pages—to this exact page with this exact verse after my simple little request reminded me once again that He is with me always, watching over me and caring for me no matter where I am or what I am doing.

Just as He cares for His smallest creatures, like the birds of the air and the lilies in the fields, He cares for me. Anything that concerns me, concerns Him. At that moment, I was filled with an indescribable peace and joy that completely enveloped my soul.

In that moment, I also recommitted my heart to the Lord. Just like the sparrow and the swallow in Psalm 84, I know that I will always make my home close to the Lord…where I know He is just a whisper away.

2

Coming to Believe

*But I did not believe what they said until I came
and saw with my own eyes...*
— *2 Chronicles 9:6*

Faith: Just Do It!

By Michael Nabi
Seattle, Washington, United States

"Faith without action is nothing." The words kept pounding in my head as the challenge to prove God existed lay before me in the form of a basketball. I was a 12-year-old, goofy, video game playing, non-athletic nerd. Although I had unwavering faith in God, I didn't know how to win arguments proving the existence of God scientifically, philosophically, or theologically, but what 12-year-old boy does?

A kid from South Africa had moved in up the street from me that school year. Speaking with a proper James Bond accent, Nigel entered my sixth grade class wearing navy blue dress pants, a button down shirt, and a blazer jacket adorned with a royal crest patch on the upper right hand pocket. "Finally!" I thought, "there's someone more nerdy than me."

It didn't take long before Nigel learned I was very outspoken about my faith. Nigel was equally outspoken; he was an atheist.

I had never met a real, living atheist. To me, they had always seemed to be "intellectual myths."

So began my quest. I would assist God in one of the great conversions of my time. Here was an atheist in my neighborhood, an oddity to my simple world. I had found a mission.

I proceeded in the customary way for a person without much experience in these situations. In my efforts to convert Nigel, I hounded him with thought-provoking questions like:

"How were we created?" "Why are we here?" "Where do we go when we die?" He would answer, and I would ponder.

After months of perpetual analysis, I concluded that atheists were simply naive. When I relayed my findings to Nigel, he found my conclusion contemptuous. Fed up with my constant pestering, Nigel decided to turn the tables on me by throwing down an athletic challenge.

"I've had quite enough of your foolish games ol' chap," he said. "Let's get down to business and tussle with a game of HORSE. If there be a God, you win. If there be no God, I win," he said emphatically.

The object of HORSE is to shoot the ball into the basket from various spots on the court without missing. For example, the first player shoots the ball toward the basket, and if he makes it, the second player then has to shoot the ball from the exact spot and use the same style of shooting the ball (whether it was underhand, overhand, or any other unique way). If he misses the basket, he gets the first letter of "H." The game continues until someone spells "HORSE," but the first player to spell "HORSE" loses!

Now that you know the objective of this game, let me explain my abilities in sports: I had NONE. And even though Nigel talked funny and dressed dopey, he was actually quite skilled at this game. The basketball match-up comparison would be like Michael Jordan playing against Bill Gates. (I would be Bill Gates.)

Like a lit firecracker ready to explode, I listened as Nigel crept closer and closer, making irritating verbal jabs like, "C'mon ol'chap. If there's a God, can't He help you beat me at a bloody game of HORSE to prove His existence?"

Suddenly, with the confidence that 10,000 angels would back me up, I blurted out, "OK, you asked for it—Bring it on!"

While I still had the floor, I proceeded to remind him of the prior agreement: "The ultimate winner has ***eternal*** bragging rights. I win—there's a God, no questions asked. You win, Nigel—there is no God whatsoever, and I will stop bugging you."

All charged up, we made our way to the basketball court to play the game of all games.

Nigel, secure in the unyielding knowledge that he reigned as a stud basketball player, conceitedly obliged to let me take the first shot.

Anticipating what God would do, I stopped and said a quick, silent prayer. Opening my eyes, I decided on a relatively simple shot from the free throw line. Releasing the ball, I methodically dribbled it a few times by my right foot that was pointed directly at the basketball hoop. Catching the ball on the third bounce, I nervously pushed it away from my chest in the direction of the basket. It hit the backboard. Bam! It hit the rim. Clunk! It did *not* go in! Oh, I was devastatingly embarrassed! Like clockwork, Nigel started in with his cruel remarks. As we battled back and forth, with my heart pounding in my chest abnormally fast, but showing calmness on my exterior, his taunts increased with every basket I would clumsily miss.

"What?" he would proclaim, "Is your God out to lunch? Is He shopping at the mall for His summer wardrobe?"

The score had racked up to a humiliating "HORS" against me while Nigel only had an "H." All he needed to do was beat me one more time to win this basketball game. As if on cue, he blurted out some of the most vulgar insults about God that I've ever heard.

I immediately froze and fervently prayed one more time. "I am sorry, God. I would never want to make You look like a fool. I don't mind looking like a fool for You, but I really need Your help right now."

Instantly, I felt God nudge me: "Go for the impossible shots."

I licked my lips, took my stance, lifted my arms, and with steady hands took my hoop shot from half court. Swish! I made it!

Nigel swaggered on up with a big arrogant grin on his face in an effort to throw off my confidence and... Kerplunk! Nigel missed.

Swish! Kerplunk!

Swish! Kerplunk!

Shot after shot, I made. He missed.

Now we were down to the final gut wrenching seconds where I had "HORS" and he had "HORS." My final shot position was all the way on the side where you could see the basket, but not the backboard, so I turned my back to the basket and pitched the ball up behind my head...

Swish! I made it!

It was Nigel's turn. Perspiring, with legs quivering, he threw the ball with a big, "Uhhh!"

Kerplunk! He missed!

The ball bounced with a thud of failure and rolled to a standstill. Silence from Nigel. No more ridiculing.

A couple of very quiet seconds went by. Then all of a sudden, Nigel exclaimed, "There must be a God! He wasn't off having tea. For you to play that way, you must have had supernatural help!"

Years later, I bumped into Nigel. He still remembers that day and the agreement he promised to honor.

Although I didn't have the best theological arguments, and I didn't know all the proper scripture verses to turn to, I had a mustard seed of faith that I put into action.

And now I know without a doubt: If we just throw the ball in faith, God's hand will score the basket.

Waking From the Dream

By Robert Baumgart
Robins Air Force Base, Georgia, United States

Not long ago, something happened that caused me to change my views from those of an atheist to a believer.

I was an atheist prior to this incident, and nothing could change my viewpoint. All of the kids at school who told me God is the only path to true happiness could not change my opinion, nor could any of the Jehovah's Witnesses who knocked at my door regularly for me to come and pray with them. The Bible, to me, was a book of pure fiction, written only to soothe the fear of death for the evolving brain.

"Just look around you," people would say, "and see the majesty of God!"

It was laughable to me then, because it was the majesty of the unknown. God, to me, was an excuse made by man to explain the unexplainable...to look more wise than those who could not understand why things are the way they are.

But my viewpoints changed drastically when something I would have considered either impossible or coincidental prior to its happening paralyzed me with fear.

Early in the morning of October 20, 1996, I awoke and stared at the ceiling. No matter how hard I tried, I could not move any part of my body. I was frozen with an unexplainable fear, and my eyes were forced to stare at my ceiling. There was something up there—not something of the physical kind, but more a feeling that there was a physical event taking place above me.

I felt the presence of two dead children hovering above me. Gradually, emerging from the darkness, two pairs of eyes began glowing in a nonexistent light. They were sad eyes, scared eyes, confused eyes that were staring into my own.

I became scared, sad, and confused as well, but I didn't know why, and I could not turn my head away from them or close my eyes to forget about them.

After what seemed like several minutes of staring, I felt one of the bodies drop from existence toward me, and my body twitched slightly for the first time since the sleep paralysis began.

Not long after the first invisible body fell toward me, the second also fell. This time, my entire body jerked forward as I leaped from my bed and screamed. I looked around my room to make sure everything was normal again. The clock read 12:10 a.m.

I decided to go get a drink, hoping it would calm my pounding heart and cool my sweating, hot body. As I left my room, my 15-year-old brother, Dan, walked toward me. "Are you okay? I heard you scream." I explained my nightmare to him and told him it was only a dream. There was nothing to worry about.

With that, Dan went back to his room to go to sleep. The dream had no meaning to me at the time.

As I went back to sleep, another dream began forming. Only a few words were popping into my head. "Jaws of life." "Three hours." And "Dead."

The words again seemed meaningless to me, but they were still disturbing, so I awoke again. This time, it was a normal waking, and the sun was shining into my bedroom window.

I walked drearily down the stairs after leaving my room and was immediately greeted by my oldest brother, Tom.

"Casey died last night," he said.

I didn't believe him, of course. It was just a sick joke. Kids don't die when they're only 15—at least not friends of the family. Tom was just fooling around.

But it occurred to me shortly after that thought that Tom would never joke around about something this serious.

"How did he die?" I asked.

"He was riding back from a party with a drunken driver and two other kids. They crashed into a tree. I talked to Mark on the phone, and he told me that they had to get him out with the jaws of life. The cops said that it took almost three hours. Casey was alive for a little while, but by the time they got to him, he was dead. The driver died on impact, and the other two lived."

I walked downstairs and, with complete disbelief, just stared blankly at the sky. There wasn't a single cloud. The birds were chirping. Everything seemed completely normal, as though nothing had really happened.

When I walked back into the house, Dan was eating a bowl of cereal, staring blankly at the table. He was still wrapped in a blanket, so I knew he had just woken. By the look on his face, I also knew that Tom had already told him about his best friend's death.

I didn't know what to say to him, so I didn't say anything. I just left the room. Dan left shortly after, stepping out onto the back patio. He left most of his cereal uneaten on the table and his blanket on the chair. The picture was very sad to me. It was empty.

I was upset about how it could have easily been Dan in the wrong place at the wrong time, and it added to the sadness I felt while looking at the half-eaten cereal.

Once my mother, a believer rather than an atheist, got home from church and heard the news, she dropped everything from her hands and ran to the back patio to comfort Dan. I ran out the front door as the realization came to me that Casey would no longer be around.

It's strange how it takes that long to realize that someone is dead after you learn of the news.

I went for a walk on this unusually warm Michigan October day. I looked around at the blue sky and again could not believe what was happening. At some point on this walk, the dream from the previous night struck me. All of the words I'd heard from Tom shed new light on this dream. Was it possible?

It wasn't until the funeral for Casey, a rainy day more appropriate for the sadness that hundreds of people were feeling, that I realized how important the dream I'd had seemed.

The newspapers said that the two boys died shortly after midnight, and I'd woken from my dream at 10 past 12:00. Tom's conversation with me had the exact same key words as my second dream included, even though Tom was on the phone downstairs, while I slept upstairs with my door closed and a fan on high power—it was impossible that I could have overheard his conversation, and the odds of it being a mere coincidence were so small that even a coincidence seemed impossible.

The only reasonable explanation that I could give myself was that somehow, something happened that science could not explain.

Somehow two people communicated to me from beyond their own lives. They were telling me that they would no longer be with us. They were scared at first, as well as confused, and sad that they would not be able to say anything to their families before they left earth. Perhaps they awoke from their own dreams, just as I had, to an unusually sunny day with chirping birds.

As odd as it sounds, this is the event that changed my beliefs from atheist to believer. I have only told a few people about this dream: my brother, my mother, and a highly religious friend of mine from high school. My brother was shocked by the accuracy of the dream. My mother and the friend were not nearly as shocked. It seemed to them, in fact, a believable event that should not make me question my own sanity. It should, rather, make me question my beliefs about life after death.

Was this event a very strange coincidence, or was it a nudge from God? I am leaning toward the latter, enjoying my new perspectives on the purpose of life and the great likelihood of life after death.

The Rose Petal

By Kelly Ann Malone
Canyon Country, California, United States

I have always felt that I am one of the fortunate ones. At a very young age, I received the answer to my prayer. I was nine at the time.

By no means was my life perfect. We didn't have much money, fancy cars, or expensive clothes. We had to make our own fun. And that we did!

On Saturday mornings, if there wasn't a wedding going on, my best friend, Marie, and I would meet up at the corner, then skip our way to our parish, St. John Baptist De La Salle, for spiritual adventures. Something about this grand structure and the ominous feeling we both got when we entered the building was unexplainable.

On Sundays, we would attend church with our parents. The church filled with hundreds of parishioners speaking in unison to the priest's commands. But there was something different about being there alone—just my friend and me. We felt we were getting special attention from the Holy Spirit. We even got the sense that the Lord was happy we were there! We had sort of a one-on-one we couldn't get through the noise of mass. We were truly searching for God's presence.

When we entered the church, we instantly felt joy and acceptance envelop our every pore. We dipped our fingers in the cool water, crossed ourselves, and felt "special."

One lovely spring afternoon, Marie and I began our usual Saturday journey. Upon entering the church, the smell of incense and candle wax, from a wedding that had taken place earlier, lingered in the aisles.

While the two of us were sitting in a pew together, I dared to initiate a question to my friend that would have a lifelong effect on both of us.

"Let's ask God for a sign of His presence," I said.

Being children, we sort of made it a game, but Jesus was very serious, thank goodness!

We structured the exact sequence of events and agreed upon the plan. We decided to go and kneel at the statue of the Virgin Mary and make our innocent plea.

Arm in arm, we slowly but excitedly moved toward the statue. With butterflies in our stomachs, we then carefully knelt down. We put our hands together in prayer and recited the *Our Father*.

Then it was time—time to test our faith. It was a child's faith, of course, but pure faith nonetheless. I did the honors.

I looked up at the beautiful statue of Mary, who had a beautiful bouquet of real red roses in her arms, and recited my prayer.

It went something like this:

"Dear Jesus. I know I am a child, but if You would give Marie and me a sign that You are real, I will never, ever, ask for another sign as long as I live. I will always know that You are real, that You love me, and that I was given the special gift of faith to carry with me for the rest of my life."

I completed my prayer, and then Marie and I looked up at the Virgin Mary and braced ourselves for our personal miracle. I could feel my heart pounding, and I am sure Marie felt the same way. We looked at each other, then back to the Blessed Mother. In less than three seconds, it happened.

One red rose petal fell from the bouquet Mary was holding! It ever so gently descended to the floor right in front of us! It was incredible!

Marie and I looked at each other in total and complete shock, mouths wide open, then ran out of the church as fast as we could! Our dear Lord must have gotten a good chuckle at the sight of us.

"Did you see that, Kelly?"

"Yes, I did. Can you believe it! We got a sign!"

We were so genuinely happy at what had just taken place. We felt so privileged and amazed that Jesus had chosen us to display His love to. We felt truly anointed and washed in the Holy Spirit. We walked a little lighter. Laughed a little harder. And prayed a little stronger. We were blessed. And we knew it.

Now, you might say it was coincidence, or even ridiculous—simply a child's fantasy or overreaction to a set of unusual circumstances. But to two 9-year-old girls, it was truly a sign.

So few times, if ever, in our lives do we look at the simple miracles happening right in front of us all the time. What we choose to believe is what transforms us. Whether it is the parting of the Red Sea, making a blind man see, or two little girls witnessing a flower petal fall from the Blessed Mother's loving arms, what we choose to take in and give us inspiration is what gives us faith.

Most people need the parting of the Red Sea to believe. And they wait all their lives for it, only to be disappointed when it does not appear. Bitter and resentful, they lose hope.

I suppose it is easier to doubt—easier to say, "Poor me. Where is my miracle?"

But all along, you have been given thousands of miracles in your life. But you gave little attention to the small details, and you could not see. With diminished hope, you could not hear.

And with little faith, you expected little. I imagine even the parting of the sea might not convince you.

As for me, I have chosen to take that tiny miracle and let it be my light. My inspiration. My gift from God. Oh, what joy and remembrance that day has given me. In times of sorrow, that rose petal has comforted me. In times of self-doubt, it has filled me with peace.

And when I come across someone in need of inspiration, it is this story that I tell.

That event was powerful enough to completely transform the rest of my life. Since that day, I have never doubted, I have never looked back and said that it was silly, and I have never again asked God to reveal himself to me. I know He is always with me.

I guess some people need the parting of the sea to become convinced Jesus is real. To me, a simple drop of a rose petal at the right time was all I needed. And I am truly grateful for that miraculous event!

Luke's Rainbow

By Steven Manchester
Sommerset, Massachusetts, United States

At one time, 11-year-old Luke Hoffman was the perfect picture of an all-American boy. He was an all-star in Fall River's Basketball League, he loved conquering the outdoors, and he saved every nickel he could for his giant trading card collection. Then, tragedy struck.

As a severe hemophiliac, Luke was diagnosed with a fairly unknown disease called AIDS. Quite painfully, life was about to change.

As a result of his courage, the love of his family, and the compassion of his town, the name "Luke Hoffman" would forever become synonymous with the word "triumph."

While Luke fought to get well, his parents, Matt and Lisa, were determined not to change anything they didn't have to. That also meant attending school. The time had come for the Fall River School Department to step up to the free throw line.

A meeting was held, where, after much debate, understanding led to compassion. Although fear was mixed in, ignorance was silenced. It was decided that Luke would continue to attend school, though his days of playing organized basketball had come to an end. It was too risky.

No matter, Fall River had still swished both free throws.

Rather than shunning an ailing boy, they embraced him. That love would unite Fall River with pride, while setting a wonderful example for the rest of the country.

A group called the "Friends of Luke" raised money. A video camera was purchased, and the most precious of memories were caught on film. Meanwhile, meals were brought to the Hoffman house, autographed sports memorabilia arrived from around the country, and The Make A Wish Foundation contacted the family. Unlike many others who requested trips to Disney World, Luke asked for and received three courtside tickets to watch the Chicago Bulls play at home. Later that trip would become the source of great spiritual comfort.

During the flight, the dying boy insisted on a window seat. The Hoffmans weren't in the air for more than five minutes when Luke hooted, "There's another one!"

Matt leaned over. "What?" he asked.

There was nothing there.

"Another rainbow!" Luke confirmed. "Don't you see it?"

Matt glanced quickly at his wife. She had the same look in her eyes. There was definitely nothing there. More than likely, the illness or the medication that fought it was making their son hallucinate, they thought.

Still, Matt couldn't lie.

"No, I don't see it," he was sorry to report.

Luke's eyes never left the window, nor did his giant smile leave his face. "I wish you did," he said, "I really wish you and Mom could both see it!"

Just prior to the start of the game, Michael Jordan sauntered over and introduced himself to Luke. It was as if the boy had just witnessed another rainbow. Luke's face literally beamed while he spoke to his hero the way someone might speak to a friend.

Matt was impressed.

The two carried on for a few brief moments. Then, as the king of the court turned to walk away, Luke blurted out a favor. "Could you hit a three-pointer for me, Mr. Jordan?"

Michael Jordan stopped, spun on his heels, and approached Luke Hoffman once more. "When I throw you a
thumbs-up, then you know that the last shot was for you!"

Luke giggled with delight. Jordan removed his embroi-
dered Chicago Bulls cap, placed it on Luke's head, and winked,
"Enjoy your show!"

To Luke's dismay, the first half of the game was close.
It seemed every one of the Detroit Pistons was on fire. Worse
yet, Michael Jordan was yet to explode. "That's OK," Luke
whispered to his dad. "Wait until you see the second half!"

The wait wasn't long. Michael Jordan stepped onto the
court like a man possessed. Before the jump ball ever landed in
his hands, he quickly turned to Luke, smiled, and winked once
more. That was it. Jordan took to the air. The arena ignited
with electricity, and Luke was on his feet for the rest of the show.

Toward the end of the last quarter, Jordan was bringing
the ball down on man-to-man coverage, but stopped just after
the half-court line. For a split second, he just seemed to stand
there and wait. A magical silence hushed the crowd. Then it
happened. To everyone's amazement, he threw the ball up and
watched.

Spinning end-over-end, the basketball seemed to float
in the air while traveling the most perfect arc. SWISH! The
crowd erupted.

Jordan turned toward courtside, smiled, and threw Luke
the signal he had promised. Matt and Lisa burst into tears. It
was like watching a miracle in the making. Luke simply returned the man's gesture, applauded, and then kneeled at his
father's side.

"Did you see it that time?" he pleaded. "Did you see the
rainbow?"

Matt nodded while Lisa pulled the boy to them. "We
did!" they swore, though this rainbow was different from others
they'd witnessed in the past. This rainbow was only orange.

The Hoffman's returned home, and Luke fought until accepting his tragic fate. On the night of his death, the boy made a promise. "When I go to heaven, I'll send you signs so you know I'm OK!"

Matt and Lisa wept and then rocked their baby into his eternal sleep.

A solid month of blinding grief passed before Matt could bring himself to visit Luke's grave. It seemed so unfair, so unnatural, that a man should bury his own son.

Lisa was relentless. Even if she wanted to, she could not deny that she felt Luke's presence in her every waking moment. Perhaps it was a mother's intuition, but she knew that Luke still had something to say. She began to convince Matt that spiritually their son had only gone to a place where he could encourage and inspire those who were not so strong.

Driving off to the cemetery, her tender words renewed a fraction of Matt's faith. Luke, however, would take care of the rest.

The sun shone down on the boy's cold stone, and Matt felt as if a sword pierced straight through his heart. He dropped to his knees and cried until the tears would no longer come. "Oh, Luke," he whimpered, "if it were only me—"

Suddenly, he saw it. It was a rainbow. Though it had not rained for days, a beautiful rainbow appeared in the distance. The sky was painted with every color in the spectrum. It lasted but a moment, and when it vanished, Matt wiped his eyes and stood.

"Did you see?" he started.

"The rainbow!" Lisa sobbed, "Luke's telling us he's OK!" The boy's wish had finally come true. His parents were no longer blind.

For better than an hour, they held each other and cried.

From that day on, when least expected, rainbows appeared in the Hoffmans' lives. After a while, they stopped asking others if they saw the same. No one ever did.

As plain as faith, though, they were there. And so was Luke.

My Father

By Glenda Thornhill Bozeman
Vinemont, Alabama, United States

It was early May, and we had just buried Daddy. He died at 2 a.m. on May 7, 1986, in the DublinVA Hospital while waiting for a heart cauterization.

I think my Daddy had to be the sweetest, gentlest man I ever knew. He was always happy and always had a big hug for you. When he got older and grayer, he use to play Santa Claus at Christmas, and he was just perfect at it.

He would cry at the sweetest things—things we take for granted everyday. Like the fact that my sister and I would come to visit and be there together at home with our families would make Daddy cry. He loved his girls and loved having us home with him and Momma.

When Daddy died, it broke my heart. I was literally sick. I couldn't believe that my Heavenly Father could take my dad away from me.

My dad had just become a Christian about six months earlier. The night he got saved, he made a conference call to my sister and me to tell us both the news. He knew we had been praying for this to happen for a long time. It was so exciting to hear him talk about the Lord and what He had done for him.

When he got saved, he "got it" from the top of his head to the tips of his toes. He began right away working for the Lord and in His house. He started tithing and going to Sunday school and cooking for different events held at the church. He witnessed and changed his life around. Others that knew him could see the change; he didn't have to tell them, but he did anyway.

I was a Christian, but still I constantly struggled—especially with hurts in my marriage. I was weak, and I guess you could say I was mad at God for "allowing" so much pain in my life, and now this—Daddy dying. It was just devastating.

I was so hurt, and then the devil started putting doubts in my mind about heaven and Daddy's salvation. Daddy was the first loved one I was close to who had died, other than my grandmother. I began to doubt whether heaven was real and wonder if his grave was his earthly home now. I wanted so not to doubt, but to believe in my faith.

We buried Dad on a Tuesday, and now it was a Saturday night. I couldn't sleep, so I stayed up late doing laundry and preparing my family's clothes for church the next day. I began talking to God and telling Him about all my doubts and fears, and all my emotions just came pouring out to Him.

Finally I decided I would make a deal with Him. I said, "God, You know I don't have any flowers in my front yard, but I need a sign that Daddy is in heaven with You and he is happy and safe. So, God, give me a flower in my yard tomorrow as a sign that he is there with You."

As soon as I had said it, a horrible, guilty feeling came over me. I knew I shouldn't be asking God for a sign and that I should just go forward on faith. But I also knew my faith was really going through a testing period, and I really wanted a sign, but I wanted even more just to trust God without question. Then I pleaded with God to forgive me for asking such a thing and for doubting my father's salvation. I even went so far as to tell Him I wouldn't even look in the yard the next day, because I was so sure Daddy was fine.

The next morning we got up to get ready for church—and with two children and a husband getting ready—just got caught up in trying to get everything just right and make it to church on time. But on the way out the door, I remembered my prayer and my "deal" with God the night before. So I held my head up high and walked to the car and got in, trying all the while not to look around the yard.

Just as we were about to pull out of the driveway, there it was—standing so tall and proud I couldn't miss it—almost as if to say, "Here I am! God sent me to you!"

I started crying, and my husband asked me if I was all right. I told him to stop the car, and I got out and pulled up this long, skinny yellow flower that was growing by the driveway just calling to me to see it.

My husband couldn't understand what was going on and why I wanted such a pitiful looking flower, but due to the circumstances, he kept quiet, and I told him I would explain everything when I could stop crying. He was as amazed as I was when I told him the whole story.

Now every time I am asked to give a witness for the Lord and what He has done for me, I always tell my flower story. It was a miracle to me—the miracle I needed to keep my faith and to get through my father's death. I knew Daddy must have told God to please send me the sign so I wouldn't fret for him. I could just see him up there looking down on me and wanting so much to tell me himself that he was okay, and that was the only way he could do it for me.

I still have the tall skinny yellow flower today. It is pressed between some wax paper, and I keep it in a special box with other memories of Daddy.

Whenever I get it out, I have to tell someone the story. It truly was a miracle from God when I needed just a little something to keep going. The devil lost his battle that day, and I regained a new found faith in God that has never left me. I vow to continue to tell my children and their children about my fathers—both of whom are in heaven—one my earthly father, and the other my Heavenly Father—who both loved me so much that they sent me a miracle so I could believe.

3

Do Unto Others

..."Love your neighbor as yourself"...
— Mark 12:31

My Husband, My Hero

By Vanessa K. Mullins
Milan, Michigan, United States

It was a Saturday afternoon, and I had deadlines to meet, but I wasn't making much progress. I kept coming up against a strong brick wall in the form of my three children. It seemed every time I sat down at the computer to write, one of the children came in with a problem: "He's being mean to me," or "She keeps changing the channel."

Before I came in to work, they were getting along fine, but it never fails that when I sit down to write, that's when they need a referee. Why couldn't they take their troubles to their Dad? I was so tired of getting up and stopping arguments, and I was getting close to that breaking point all parents reach sooner or later.

It must have been obvious to my husband, Gary, because he stepped in to help. Even though he wasn't feeling too well that day, he decided I needed a break and that he would take the kids somewhere to get them out of my hair and give me a chance to finish my work.

He showered, dressed, and told the kids to get ready because they were going out and giving mom some time to herself. It was also a great opportunity for some daddy and kids time together, as it had been a while since they were able to go out together "without Mom," due to work and other things that sometimes get in the way of family time.

The four of them decided they would go to Toledo, which is about 30 miles south of us. They wanted to go shopping, out to lunch, and just spend a nice day together. Since they were going a bit of a distance, Gary decided to gas up the car before leaving town, and they stopped at a local gas station to fill up the tank. As our kids sat in the car listening to music or talking—or whatever it is kids do when their parents are not in the car—Gary stood outside filling up the tank with gasoline.

A small dark pickup truck pulled up and parked by the pump next to the one my husband was using. Gary heard the truck door next to him close, and then he heard a tapping noise coming from the direction of the pickup. He turned to see two small children in the truck who were tapping on the window, playing, and trying to get his attention. The window was slightly cracked, so he could hear them talking to him, laughing, and playing. He smiled and waved back at them and made them laugh—the way most good dads do with kids.

When the gas tank was filled, Gary turned away for a moment to remove the hose and replace it on the pump, then close the gas cap. At the same time, he looked at our children sitting in the car, but he saw something in the reflection of our car window that caught his eye. The truck behind him was slowly moving away.

He knew something wasn't right. He didn't remember hearing the mother come out of the station and get into the truck, so he knew the children were in the vehicle alone. As he turned to look, he saw the truck picking up speed as it began to roll down the hill (that the gas station sits on) out into the four-lane road full of afternoon traffic.

He didn't know it at the time, but apparently, while the children were playing, they had knocked the truck out of gear. Their mother had no idea her children were in danger.

With no regard for his own safety, my husband ran after the truck into the busy four-lane street. Other cars sped by the small truck, honking their horns and not paying any attention to who was inside.

The pickup neared the opposite side of the street, with oncoming traffic just a short distance away, just as Gary reached the truck, yanked open the door, somehow got his foot inside, and stepped on the brakes.

By this time, the children were frightened, crying, and screaming. Gary calmed them and assured them that he was going to help them and that their mommy was in the store, but that she would be out in a moment. Gary is really good with kids, and they believed him and stopped crying. He told them to sit still while he got out and got their truck out of the street. Amazingly, they did, even not knowing what was happening or where their mommy was.

Gary started to push the truck back up the hill by himself. Meanwhile, drivers on the four-lane street sped by in both directions, honking their horns, screaming obscenities at him, and yelling for him to get his truck out of the street. As he pushed the truck out of the street, out of the many, many cars that passed by, only one other man stopped to help him.

At this point, the children's mother noticed the commotion, saw her truck in the middle of the street being pushed by two men, and ran out of the store. She ran to the truck, offered a slight thanks to my husband, and then got into her car and sped away.

On this particular day, Gary was a hero, not only to me, for giving me the time and space I needed to finish my work, but also to two small children and their family. We will never know what might have happened to those two precious children if Gary hadn't been there—at the right time and in the right place—or what might have happened to others who could have been hurt, as well. Who knows how many people were blessed by the nudges that directed Gary that day?

A Name Without A Face

By Linda Adams
Arlington, Virginia, United States

On occasion, a single event can remind us of the impact we have on other people's lives. Sometimes it might be as simple as smiling at a stranger and making them feel good. Such an event, seemingly insignificant at the time, happened to me, but without a gentle nudge from God, I might not have done it.

It came in the form of a greeting card for a co-worker, sitting on my chair when I came back from lunch. The card was brightly colored with a bouquet of flowers on the front and a yellow sticky note attached to it. The note indicated that the card was being passed around for one of my co-workers, Mary Bishop, who had been hospitalized.

My first instinct was to give the card to the next person. Sure, I recognized Mary's name—I'd seen it on the department phone list just below my name. But I didn't know her. I didn't even know what she looked like or where her cube was.

And here was this card, full of cheerful greetings from co-workers she was friends with. What should I do? Should I sign it? Or should I leave the space for someone who at least knew what she looked like? It seemed that nearly everyone else had already signed it; there was only a little bit of room left.

It was a question I couldn't answer at that moment, so I set the card aside. Two hours later, I caught sight of the card again, and I found myself reaching for it without really thinking about it.

There was a small bit of space near the bottom—enough room for a short message. But what should I write? Most of the other messages were more personal, and because I didn't know her, everything I came up with sounded wrong.

Finally, I decided to keep it simple and wrote, "I hope you get well soon." That didn't really sound good to me, but it was the best I could come up with. Even as I signed it, I felt like a fraud, signing a card for someone I didn't know.

A week later, I received an email message about Mary. She was still in the hospital and very ill. The email was fairly vague about what was happening. That wasn't a good sign.

Another week passed, and I received another email message on Mary's condition. Again, it was vague about how she was doing. It did say that she was in good spirits and was looking forward to her birthday in two days.

The next day, she died. She was only 43.

I found out through email.

I sat back and looked at the message for a long time. This was a person who worked in my department—in the same cube farm—who had just died, and I didn't know what she looked like. I searched my memory for her face, oddly feeling desperate to remember any detail. Surely I must have passed her in the aisles or washed hands next to her in the bathroom. But there was still no face—just the name.

The company scheduled a memorial service for her in one of the larger conference rooms, and everyone in the department was invited.

Once again, as I looked at the notice about the service, the same doubts went through my mind. Memorial services were to help family members and friends have a sense of closure following a death. I was neither. Still, a part of me felt I should go.

On the day of the memorial, a crisis erupted at work. I had an extremely short deadline of only a couple hours, and it needed to be met. I looked at the clock. I might not make the memorial service. As I worked on the project, I became aware that I was angry at the thought of not going. I needed to go.

Suddenly, at 10 minutes to, I had everything resolved, and I found myself headed upstairs.

Another nudge? Perhaps.

I stopped just inside the door, feeling as if everyone was looking at me. There were about 50 people seated inside, but the room was silent. When they spoke, it was in hushed whispers.

I paused to scan all those faces—some I knew and some I didn't—and wondered if they knew what a fraud I was. I was probably the only one there who'd never even spoken to Mary. Still, I sat in the front row, on the end.

The family minister had agreed to deliver the eulogy for the employees. I listened at first, but my mind drifted. I felt so uncomfortable being here that it was difficult for me to concentrate.

Then the minister started to explain what Mary had gone through in her last weeks. His words pulled me in and kept me there.

Mary hadn't been feeling well for about a month and had finally gone to her doctor, he told us. The doctor admitted her to the hospital for some tests and discovered a brain tumor. They began treatment, but it was already too late. The tumor was extremely aggressive, and in the last week of her life, it had left her unable to talk.

"But," the minister said, his gaze sweeping the audience, taking in every face, "she didn't let it get her down. She was so happy when she received that card from all of you, reading everything you said. She couldn't say anything, but she could still smile, and she was smiling. You helped her in her time of need."

It was as if he had spoken directly to me. I straightened up as the words settled in. Like that smile to a stranger having a bad day, my message on that card had given her something important—something she needed. She had known, when she saw that card, that she wasn't alone.

Even though I hadn't known her, I had been there when she needed me.

Prescription for Peace

By Johnnie Ann Burgess Gaskill
Thomaston, Georgia, United States

L ate one evening, my younger daughter and I sat down at
the kitchen table for a snack. Just after we'd seated ourselves, I remembered that the day's mail lay unopened in another room. Although my tired body yearned to stay put, I forced
myself to get up and get the mail. As I sorted through it, I noticed a hand-addressed envelope bearing the return address of
our family doctor. *Hmm,* I thought, *Whatever can this be about?*

Leaving all the other mail behind, I took the letter to the
kitchen table and sat down. Noting the bewilderment the letter
was causing me, Jena asked, "Who's the letter from, Mom?"

I answered her by stating the name of one of our physi-
cians.

Looking surprised and puzzled, she asked, "Why'd we
get a letter from *him*?"

"Give me a minute, and we'll find out."

She watched my face carefully as I read the one-page,
handwritten letter. I looked up, my eyes brimming with tears,
and said, "One day, Honey, I'm going to learn that obedience
brings blessing."

"What are you talking about?" Jena asked.

"A couple of months ago," I said, "I was given a pam-
phlet containing 60 ideas for sharing the Gospel. As I looked
over the list, I felt drawn to the one encouraging me to send a

note to a doctor thanking him for his services and assuring him that I was praying for him."

"So you chose Dr. Smith*?" she said, trying to move the story along.

"I did, for you know how wonderful he has been to us, how he has gone above and beyond what others doctors would do."

She nodded.

"Well, Honey, you know me! I thought about it for several weeks before I finally took the time to write it. I felt guilty about waiting so long, especially since the actual writing didn't take long at all. Now, after reading his response to me, I'm *glad* I procrastinated."

I read the letter again.

"Jena," I exclaimed, shaking my head, "I just can't believe this."

By that time, Jena was thoroughly confused!

"Please, Mom, just read it to me," she said as she continued to eat her snack.

I began, but could hardly continue when I came to this part: "I was having probably the worst week of my life last week when I finally found your letter at the bottom of my mail stack. After reading it, I told [my partner] that God must have known I needed a lift, and you were His answer...your note couldn't have come at a better time."

Jena and I sat for several minutes in silence. I read the three paragraphs in the letter again and again and felt so touched that the doctor had taken time out of a busy schedule to thank me and to share a bit of his heart, for we were strangers, except for what we'd learned about one another during the visits my daughters and I had made to his medical office. I could only conclude that my having shared a bit of what was in my heart helped him share his feelings with me.

As I reflected on his words, one sentence stood out: "...God must have known I needed a lift and you were His answer."

Tears filled my eyes. I thought, *Thank You, Father, for the inexpressible joy of knowing You used me to give Dr. Smith a lift when he was really down. Thank You for patiently reminding me again and again to write the note. Thank You for not allowing me to avoid the 'assignment' You impressed upon my mind and heart, even though I procrastinated many days, hoping all the while that You would let me off the hook. Even so, Your timing was amazingly perfect! Thank You for teaching me that obedience to You does bring blessing—to me, as well as to others.*

I sat in absolute awe of how God had taken my one teeny-tiny act of obedience—delayed though it was—and used it to powerfully affect a fellow struggler. I remembered the principle that—with God's help—our little becomes much. Then I asked, "Father, how many others have You wanted to touch through me? Yet, how many people have missed the encouragement and comfort You wanted them to have because I failed to respond to Your gentle but persistent nudges?"

As I asked God to forgive me for blocking the blessings He intended for others, I also prayed He would help me, from that day forward, to allow His love to flow freely from me to others, just as He desires it to do.

*Name has been changed

Phone Call From God

By Bonnie Compton Hanson
Santa Ana, California, United States

"You're having surgery when? OK, I'm marking it on my calendar right now. Tell Don we'll be right there with him in the waiting room."

As dozens of friends and family members called with that same message, I had visions of so many visitors at the hospital that they'd have to take numbers to get a seat. But that was good. It's scary facing breast cancer surgery. How wonderful to be so loved! How Don would enjoy all their support!

Then the week before my scheduled date, I called my surgeon's office to make sure I knew all the instructions I would need to follow.

"Arrive at the Outpatient Pavilion next Wednesday at 12:00 noon," the nurse said. "You'll have some tests first. The surgery itself is scheduled for 4:15 p.m. Nothing to eat or drink after midnight Tuesday night except for your normal pills. Bring loose clothing to wear. You'll go home that same evening; someone will need to drive you. Got all that?"

"Yes, thanks." Simple enough.

In fact, since the hospital was only half an hour from home, I'd have plenty of time to teach my 10:00 a.m. Bible class that morning before leaving. Perfect! The fellowship of the Word and the class members would be a "warm fuzzy" comfort for me before the trying time ahead.

Then I received still another phone call. "Bonnie, we heard about your surgery. We'll be at the hospital at three to see you before you go under. Take care."

Yes, a call similar to the others—but different enough to put me in a panic. For this one was from a relative who loved me dearly—but who had long held a grudge against my husband, Don. In fact, he had neither seen nor spoken to Don for nearly 37 years, until my mother's funeral the previous spring. What if he got into an argument with Don in the waiting room and made a big scene in front of all my friends who'd promised to be there?

I sadly called back my friends. "Uh—look," I stammered, "it might just be better if you didn't come. Thanks anyway." Then I prayed to God not to let my worst fears happen.

The next Monday at 6:30 p.m., just before leaving the house for a meeting, I got still another call. "This is the hospital," said the crisp voice at the other end. "We want to make sure you have all the instructions for your surgery Wednesday."

So I recited all the directions that I had written down.

"Good, good. And do you know what time to check in?"

"Yes, 12:00 noon."

"At 12:00? Oh, no! Who in the world told you that? You need to be here no later than 11:00 a.m." That meant I'd have to cancel the Bible class after all. No Bible class, no hospital full of friends. *God,* I sighed, *this just doesn't seem fair!*

That Wednesday, Don and I dutifully arrived at the hospital at 11:00 a.m. and signed in. When the receptionist saw my name, she frowned. "What are you doing here so early, Mrs. Hanson?" she asked. "You're not supposed to be here till 1:00 p.m."

"Now wait a minute!" I protested. "Someone from this hospital called Monday evening at 6:30 and told me to be here at 11:00 this morning."

"Impossible!" she huffed. "The office that makes those calls is never open later than 5:00 p.m."

By now I was getting a little testy, too.

"But I did get a call. If not from your office, then who called me?"

"I don't know," she answered. "But I'll find out." So while I waited, she contacted several people in her office, then in my surgeon's office, and then in my regular physician's office.

Finally she announced, "Just as I said, Mrs. Hanson, no one called you. It was all your imagination. So you can go back home and return at 1:00 p.m. or sit here and wait."

"But I did get that phone call!" I insisted. Steaming, I returned to my seat. I had to miss my Bible class, I had to miss my friends, I was full of dread about my relative's coming, and I was starving and had to miss lunch. I wasn't looking forward to the surgery and all its pain. I couldn't have been more miserable. And now to be insulted like this!

A few minutes later, a kind nurse said, "Mrs. Hanson, since you're here early, we might as well go ahead anyway and do all your tests."

Unfortunately, those tests were extremely painful. But both the nurse and the attending physician were very sympathetic and said they'd be praying for me.

When I finished, another nurse rushed in. "Guess what, dear? The surgery before yours has been canceled. Since you're here and your tests are already done, the doctor can take you at 2:00 p.m. instead of 4:15 p.m.!"

I had already asked my friends not to come. My family, except for Don, wouldn't be here until 5:00 p.m. But my relative and his wife were coming at 3:00 p.m. So I'd be in surgery when they arrived—and not able to act as a peacemaker between them and Don. *Dear God*, I prayed frantically as the anesthetic took hold, *I know You're in the miracle business. We sure could use one right now!*

When I came to, I was conscious of laughing voices and smiling faces—Don, my relative, and his wife! All standing side by side like old friends, joking and telling stories. Impossible! I opened my eyes in wonderment. "Since you were in surgery when they got here," Don explained, "we all went out to lunch together."

"And had a great time," my relatives laughed. Then they gave me a toy "angel" bear, flowers, and lots of hugs and kisses. And, oh, so much more! For what an amazing thing God had done! If I hadn't gone to the hospital early and, thus, had my surgery early, they wouldn't have been thrown together for lunch—just the three of them—and, with God's help, erased that barrier of 37 years as if it never existed. And, of course, I wouldn't have gone in early if I hadn't received that phone call—the phone call that the hospital insisted "nobody made."

But that God of miracles had planned long before to help heal not just my physical problems, but the sad rift in our family as well. Oh, what a wonderful God we have!

Reach Out and Live

By Leigh Platt Rogers
Benicia, California, United States

When I transferred to the College of William and Mary in Williamsburg, Virginia, I was very much on my own. As a transfer student, I was not able to find housing on campus and, therefore, found myself living alone in a small apartment about three miles away. I felt small, lost, alone, and disoriented.

But that was not the real problem that sophomore year. The year before, as a freshman at a "party" school in Florida, I had felt under extreme pressure to "fit in" with the tan, thin, and beautiful dream girls I saw all around me. I tried diet after diet to keep my weight down—and I was not fat—but I felt this need to have the perfect body.

After I'd been in Florida for a full semester struggling with schoolwork and social pressures, I discovered a miraculous way to be able to eat anything I wanted and not gain a pound. Today it is called bulimia and is a recognized, worrisome eating disorder.

Eating disorders are strange, mysterious, and insidious. In the beginning, I felt I was completely in control over what I could eat. Unlike the anorexic who starves herself, I did not become significantly thin. I was eating plenty, so I looked "normal."

Of course, I always had to leave the table after eating to go to the bathroom. Soon the binging and purging cycles started to happen more and more often. Every morning I would wake up and promise myself that I would not eat "too much," so I would not feel like I had to purge, but every day I broke that promise.

I found myself caught in a vicious world of abnormality and unreality.

My story with my friend, Jessica*, starts when I met her during an initiation into a sorority at William and Mary. We, as pledges, were told to dress in our initiation outfits. We began to strip off our t-shirts as directed and put on the white gowns. As I dressed, I happened to glance over at Jessica, who was next to me, and drew in my breath with horror. Shock coursed through my body, as I could easily see every single rib bone and the sunken shape of her stomach. She was terribly thin—almost skeletal—and reminded me of the pictures I had seen of prisoners of war.

Instinctively, I knew there was something wrong with her, and I also realized that her problem was not much different from my own.

That night, after our initiation ceremony, we were celebrating and toasting each other with champagne. Having had nothing to eat, the alcohol I imbibed went straight to my head and loosened my tongue. I put my glass together with Jessica's and leaned forward. I whispered in her ear, "There's something wrong with you." Alarmed, she drew back sharply, and I saw the fear in her eyes.

I said, "I know because there is something wrong with me, too." She stared at me, and her hollow face and tortured eyes spoke of her pain. Silently, she moved away and avoided me.

The next time I saw Jessica was about two weeks later. I ran into her while walking to class. She carried a backpack and was walking rather slowly. As soon as she saw me, she averted her eyes, and I think she would have passed by if I had not said, "Hey, Jessica, I'm sorry I scared you."

I took a deep breath, because it looked like she was going to ignore me, but to my relief, she looked directly at me and stopped. Her shoulders slumped, and suddenly she looked exhausted.

"It's OK," she said.

I hesitantly said, "Look, I spoke the truth, but I was not trying to scare you or make you mad. I saw you at the initiation. I know you have a problem, but I have one, too. You're not alone."

Suddenly she opened up and blurted out that she was on her way to see a therapist. Her mother was threatening to take her out of school if she did not gain some weight. I told Jessica I thought I should be in therapy, too, because I was also fighting a horrible problem with food. I told her I was scared all the time. I saw relief in her face and gratefulness at my honesty in her eyes.

By the end of the semester, we had become good friends. I was able to move onto campus for the second semester into a dorm across from Jessica's. We slowly got to know each other better. It is interesting, however, that the eating disorder—which was overwhelmingly controlling our lives—was a subject we avoided discussing. It was "taboo" until one memorable day.

It was a gorgeous, sunny spring day. After my morning classes, I raced back to my dorm to don my swimsuit and begin working on my tan. I headed to a favorite grassy spot between our two dorms and laid out my blanket. I sighed with happiness as I felt the warmth of the sun. Perfect.

A few minutes later, I felt a shadow. Jessica was standing there in her jogging shorts and t-shirt, covered in sweat. I shaded my eyes to see her better and started to say, "hi," but before the word could leave my lips, she fell to her knees, and I saw her clearly. She was in a complete and utter panic. Her eyes were filled with tears, and her mouth trembled. She was shaking like a leaf.

I grabbed her hands, which were ice-cold. I said, "Jessica! What is it?"

She swayed back and forth, shaking her head. She could not speak.

I was getting scared. "Jessica! What is wrong?" I shook her hands and raised my voice, feeling the beginning of panic in myself. "What? What is wrong? *Tell me!*"

She tore her hands from mine and covered her face. She began to cry in earnest, and between heaving sobs, she said, "I want to die."

Stunned, I said stupidly, "What?"

She pulled her hands from her face, and I saw an agony so great that my heart hurt with grief for her pain.

I felt my own tears beginning to well up as I heard her say clearly, "I just want to die. I'm going to kill myself. I can't take it anymore."

My mind was reeling, and I had no idea what to say. What do you say to someone who is in such pain that they want to die?

I was also afraid, you see. Afraid of saying the wrong thing. Afraid that she really meant it.

I knew why she wanted to—I had experienced my own inner desperation and despair.

I opened my mouth and said the first thing that came to mind: "Well, you just can't."

It was her turn to look at me blankly. It was probably not what she expected to hear.

I said, "Jessica, you can't die. I need you. You're all I have."

I took her in my arms and hugged her tight. I said over and over, "You're my only friend. You can't leave me here alone. We have each other. We can help each other. We can get better."

And she cried in my arms like a tired, scared, exhausted child.

That moment was a changing point for both of us. I did not realize how close I had come to losing my dear friend until she told me later that she had had her suicide all planned out. She'd been planning it for weeks. She had attended her classes as usual that morning and then got ready for her daily run. She had had a razor ready. She knew what to write in her note. And when she was done with her jog, she had planned on going to her room to take a bath with the razor.

It was when she got back from her jog and was walking to her dorm that suddenly her resolve crumbled and she felt something drawing her to the other side of the dorm where I was getting ready to sunbathe.

Then when she saw me, she hesitated, but there was this strong force that moved her forward and kept her walking towards me. She hadn't planned to talk to me—but thank goodness she did.

To this day, I thank the Lord for His help. Had it not been for a sunny day, had I not decided to sunbathe, and had Jessica not seen me, I might have lost her.

Somehow she found the strength to reach out for her life. Together we were able to help each other through some difficult times.

We each sought additional help through therapy. The closer we became, the more I helped Jessica see that life was worth living—and she gave me the strength to acknowledge that I did not have to be perfect.

Today, thanks to the Lord, we continue to have a loving and close friendship that I would not give up for anything.

*Name has been changed to protect her privacy

Please, God, Just Let Her Get Better

By Shelley Ann Wake
Aberglasslyn, NSW, Australia

One day my mother got sick and just didn't get better again. She went to hospital for a simple little operation, but she came home with an infection.

I rang home that night, expecting my dad to tell me she was home and better now. Instead, he told me she was sick, probably from the anesthetic. I told him to give her my love and I would call again tomorrow.

I called the next day, expecting to be told she was better now—she had slept it off. Instead, I was told she was still sick—vomiting all the time—and they were going back to see the doctor.

That night my dad told me that my mother had an infection, but she had antibiotics now and would start to get better soon.

This was the story for the next few weeks—calling and visiting just waiting for her to get better. She was always supposed to get better the next day or after a few days or after a good night's rest, but she didn't.

Two weeks later she was back in hospital having an operation to find the source of the infection. And then it started again. My dad told me the doctors were sure they had found the problem, and she would be fine now.

Yet another two weeks later she was back in hospital having another operation to find the source of another infection.

She went home after that, and she got a little better. But only a little better. She was well enough that she didn't sleep all of the time. And she was well enough to sit in bed and talk or read or watch movies. But she never got "all better."

The sickness was gone now, but it was like it had left a shadow behind, a shadow that kept her in the dark now. She didn't smile so much anymore. She talked now as if she was tired all the time. She didn't laugh at all.

And sometimes, when she was talking, it was like little tears were sitting right there on the edge. It was like she was not game to cry those tears in case she wouldn't be able to stop crying. So she just sat there on the edge, not happy and not sad, but somewhere in between.

And no matter what I did for her, she never seemed to cheer up. I bought her presents, I sat and told her funny stories, and I tried to comfort her, but it was like she was looking at me through a fog.

And then she got worse. Then the place she had been sitting at between happiness and sadness became sadness. She told me she was so sick of herself—that she just wanted to get away from herself, but she couldn't. She told me she hated the fact that she couldn't seem to get better. She told me she hated herself for making all of us worry about her.

Her pet dog, the dog that she cared for as much as any dog can be cared for, jumped into the bed and snuggled up next to her. She looked at the dog with such sadness and said to me, "I can't pat the dog anymore, because I don't want to give my sadness to him."

She went to the doctor that week, and he gave her medication for depression. The doctor explained to us how there had been a certain toll on her mind because of all the sickness, and it was not something she could just snap out of it. She took her medication, and we waited for her to get better. But the only real change we saw was that she slept more. And that she seemed even further away when we spoke to her.

I have prayed before, idle prayers that don't quite have my whole heart. But this was different. I knelt down, and I didn't just pray for God to help my mother, I begged for Him to help my mother.

I went to see her the next day. She sat there in bed, and I sat there and talked to her. I begged her to talk to me, to tell me what was wrong, to let me help her.

She just looked at me blankly. She just looked at me and did nothing. Not a word, not a shrug, not a gesture, not any reaction at all.

Everything about her said, *I just couldn't be bothered anymore.*

Sitting there, waiting for something to happen to make her better, I heard a little voice in my head. That little voice was telling me to tickle her. I just brushed away the thought, know- ing it was not the appropriate thing to do in this situation. But I heard that voice again, a voice somewhere inside telling me to tickle her.

Without a clue of what I was doing, and without even considering it, I leapt into my mother's bed, and I dug my fin- gers lightly into her ribs. At first she did nothing—just lay there.

But I kept at it, and the next thing I knew, she squirmed a bit. And then she let out a little squeal. And that squeal turned into a laugh. She sat there hugging her ribs and laughing for what seemed like hours. And somewhere in there, I hugged her, and that laughter turned to tears. She sat there with her head on my shoulder and cried. And somewhere in all those tears, she let go of her fear, and she let go of her sadness.

And from that one moment, she became herself again. Not completely and not all at once, but from that day, she started to climb out of her sadness. And sometimes, when she slips down into that sadness again, I say, "Mom, I'll tickle you," and she smiles.

Dad asked me after that day what on earth made me decide to tickle her. I told him it was just a little voice inside of me I decided to listen to.

"Whatever it was," he said, "Thank you."

Thanks to that voice, and the fact that I listened to it, we have my mum back now. And I have never been so grateful.

God at Work

By Louise Classon
Gaithersburg, Maryland, United States

I am a freelance writer with a home office. On a Tuesday in 1996, I was diagnosed with a rare disease, an arteriovenous malformation (AVM) of the brain. Because I was upset about the diagnosis, I decided not to take any business calls on the following day. I turned on the answering machine, pulled the covers over my head, and decided to have a pity party. That lasted until 1:00 p.m. when the phone rang and I decided to go into the office to see who was calling. I heard a business acquaintance start to leave his name, and I decided on the spur of the moment to pick up the phone and take the call.

The phone call was from the president of a snack food company wanting to know when the article I had written about his company would appear in a magazine. I gave him the information and proceeded to tell him I had just been diagnosed with a rare disease.

I was appalled that I had blurted out this information to a man I had only spoken to twice before and in a strictly professional manner.

However, I remembered that at the end of our second interview, he had indicated that he believed the success of his company was due to his belief in God and to the fact that the principals of the company started each day in prayer. At the time, his comment struck me as straightforward and sincere.

In over 10 years of interviewing businessmen for trade journal articles, that had been the first time anyone made a comment about the relevance of his faith in his business life. At the time, I told him that I, too, believed in the power of prayer. And his faith had stuck in my mind. When he called me on this particular Wednesday, it was the recollection of the second conversation that I had had with him that spurred me into sharing my diagnosis with him.

He admitted that on that particular day, he had been nudged by God to call me. The thought that he should check up on the progress of the article came to him several times during that morning. Finally, he obeyed the urging.

After I shared my diagnosis with him, he said that he and the principals of his company would pray for me each morning. As an encouragement, he said that his father-in-law had been diagnosed with a brain tumor a couple of years earlier and was now doing well. He said he believed that daily prayer and good medical treatment both had a positive effect in reducing the size of his father-in-law's tumor.

The man urged me to seek a prayer community, be anointed with oil, and be prayed for by the elders of the church.

This conversation provided encouragement and direction at a time when I was floundering. I took his advice and found a prayer group in my local area and began attending weekly meetings. In addition, I received the sacrament of the sick from a Roman Catholic priest. I am Roman Catholic, and this is a sacrament that involves anointing the recipient with holy oil. I now also attend mass and read scripture daily.

Who would have thought that a simple conversation with a business contact—a virtual stranger—would be the first step in my establishing a personal relationship with the Lord? It started a faith journey for me that has resulted in spiritual, emotional, and physical healing.

Picking up the phone on that Wednesday is only the first of many nudges I have received from the Lord since my diagnosis. I have also followed the Lord's urging with regard to medical treatment.

Because of the nature of the diagnosis, I sought medical evaluation from three world class hospitals in the Baltimore/ Washington D.C. area. None of the doctors agreed about the type of treatment needed. So with God's urging, I sought medical evaluation at a hospital in New York City. In a cab, on the way to being evaluated in New York, I got an overwhelming feeling of peace. I met with the doctors, heard what they had to say, and told them I would think about their treatment option.

As we were leaving that hospital, I told my husband that I had finally found the right medical treatment for my disease. The sense of God's peace was an important factor in my decision.

Since my diagnosis in 1996, I have had seven cerebral angiograms and six embolization procedures. The embolization procedures involve threading a catheter from an entry point in my leg up to my brain and inserting a compound to block off abnormal blood vessels. In 2000, I had gamma knife surgery that involves focusing 201 points of radiation on one spot in the brain. The last cerebral angiogram I had in 2001 showed no new AVMs, and I don't need to undergo another cerebral angiogram until 2003.

I am confident that the Lord led me to the correct medical treatment. He heals, not only directly, but most often through the use of medical personnel and other people He puts in our path.

I have received many healing blessings since I took the nudge to answer the phone on that Wednesday afternoon. Since then, I have received spiritual and emotional healing and the discernment to find the correct medical intervention for my rare disease.

But even more important than all the healing blessings, is the personal relationship I have developed with the Lord. The Lord is now central to all aspects of my life, and I am sharing His blessings with others by participating in prayer team ministry—a trained team that prays with people seeking healing in their lives.

I will always be thankful to this business associate for starting me on this faith-filled path. He followed a nudge to make a phone call and to share his faith with me.

For my part, I am grateful that I followed the Lord's urging to take that phone call and to seek medical treatment beyond my local area.

Throughout this whole experience, I see God working through other people in my life and even using AT&T to accomplish His miracles.

4

With God All Things Are Possible

Jesus looked at them and said, "With man this is impossible, but not with God; all things are possible with God."

— *Mark 10:27*

The Unexpected Flight

By Vanessa Bruce Ingold
Fullerton, California, United States

I was a 20-year-old hair stylist when I moved to Long Beach, California. I couldn't wait to leave Lafayette, Louisiana. Having been born there, it was the only place I had ever lived. I had never been to any other states, except Texas and Mississippi, and I wanted to live near the ocean and be in a big city. I wanted to go to the mountains. I wanted to experience a hot desert day, yet end with a cold desert night. *California has it all*, I thought.

Boredom was not the only reason I left. I had no family ties to keep me there. My parents had divorced when I was five, and I had never a very close relationship with either parent. So I had moved out when I was 18. My older brother, Britton, and older sister, Pam, had moved out at 18, also. Since they had left, we had grown apart. I left Louisiana when my brother was 26 and my sister was 23.

I was excited to begin a new life in Southern California. I thought that after leaving Louisiana and moving away from my friends, that I would be able to quit my party lifestyle. I had started drinking when I was 16 years old. After turning 18, I was constantly at nightclubs where I drank and did drugs.

However, I was not less tempted in California. Nor did I have greater will power to say no to the things I wanted to quit.

On January 23, 1992, about two weeks after my 23rd birthday, I lay in bed crying. I had spent my lonely Christmas high on drugs, and I was missing my family.

"God, please change me."

I was scared of dying and I wanted assurance to know I would go to heaven.

The very next morning, I was in a traumatic bicycle accident. I swerved away from a car door being opened in the parking lane and rode straight into oncoming traffic.

I was run over by all four wheels of a Ford Ranger truck, and every long bone in my body was broken, except one, which totaled 111, and the mitral valve in my heart was ripped.

Amazingly, I had no head trauma. Although I was in and out of shock, in the emergency room, I gave a doctor my friend's phone number. My friend then gave the number of the hair salon I was working at. The owner of the salon provided the emergency contact phone numbers that were listed in my work file.

A nurse from Long Beach Memorial Hospital urgently, yet calmly, tried to explain the severity of the accident to my brother, who was a paramedic.

"It is obvious that the truck ran over her, because she has tire tracks going across her chest at an angle, starting at the left side. Her heart has been punctured and her mitral valve is severely ripped. It is hanging like a thread, but the doctors are trying to prolong replacing it. Because of the multitude of injuries and blood loss, they don't think she'll make it through heart surgery."

My mom, brother, sister, and dad took the first flight possible. My mom and brother almost missed their flight at the layover in Texas. The pilot from Louisiana contacted the pilot in Texas before Britton and Mom got off the plane.

"I have a couple of people here who are gonna be a few minutes late getting to your plane. Can you wait? Over and out."

"Not a problem," the California bound pilot replied.

Britton and Mom arrived at the hospital at 7:30 p.m. that Friday night. Pam and Dad arrived later.

I had a heart attack two days later.

"Vanessa probably will not make it through the surgery, but she will certainly die if we do nothing," Dr. McConnell, my heart surgeon, told my family.

Six months later, I walked out of that hospital smiling, with a pig valve in my heart.

Recovery was not easy. Though no scars were on my face, the many scars on the rest of my body showed what I had been through. But after not having talked to my family since I had moved to California, receiving their support had encouraged me. The accident had drawn us together. What the enemy tried to use for evil, God had used for good. He was changing tragedy in my life to something good.

My mother tried to persuade me to move back to Louisiana, but I still loved California and had much support from friends in Long Beach. Six months after being released from the hospital, I started going to Long Beach City College, because I did not want to continue as a hairstylist.

My mother was born and raised in Germany, and all of my family on my mother's side lived there. They had been praying for my recovery. My dad was born and raised in Texas, so my relatives there were also praying for me. Actually, my Texan grandparents had been praying for me since they had become Christians, which had been a few years after my parent's divorce. They had prayed that I would not only have a relationship with my father on earth, but also with my Father in Heaven.

Six months after I had been out of the hospital, and as a full-time student, I began my relationship with my Father in Heaven. My friend, whom I had worked with at the hair salon before the accident, invited me to church. She and the women's Bible study group had been praying for me.

"Whoever wants to receive Jesus Christ as Lord and Savior today, come to the front, and we'll pray for you," the pastor said after he had finished the Bible study.

Since we were sitting in the front row, all I had to do was stand up and take a few steps. There my Savior met me.

"*And we know that all things work together for good to those who love God, to those who are called according to His purpose,*" the pastor read from Romans Chapter 8, as I sat in church the following Sunday.

That is the Scripture of my life, I thought.

****

A year later, during Christmas vacation, I took a flight from Long Beach, California, to Louisiana. I had not visited since I had moved.

"Whoever would like to delay their flight a couple of hours will receive a travel voucher," I heard through the airport's loudspeaker at my layover in Dallas, Texas.

As a full-time student without much income, I was the first at the service counter. It was only a one-hour wait, and I was happy to ride on a 747 that had many empty seats, so it was not crowded like the flight I would have taken.

"I guess I should use this voucher during spring break, but God, should I use it to visit Louisiana again or family in Texas or my friend in Arizona?" I wondered during the plane ride.

I had a joyful reunion with family and friends. I had hoped that my grandparents would be able to visit with us in Louisiana, but they were not able to. However, it was a joy for me to tell Grandma and Grandpa on the phone that I was now a Christian, thanks to their prayers.

"Do you have any bubble gum?" my grandfather teased as I spoke to him on the phone. I laughed as I remembered the last time I had shown off my huge bubbles to him when I was five years old.

After two weeks, I returned home to California.

A month later, as I sat talking to roommates, the phone rang. It was my Aunt Celestine. She had bad news.

"Grandpa died this morning," she told me. "Grandma Bruce found him lying in the garden. We all are shocked, since he has not had any health problems. Can you come to Texas for his funeral? You can stay with Grandma Bruce. Your dad, brother, and sister will be flying in from Louisiana. There's plenty of room at Grandma Bruce's house for you all."

My mind rapidly tried to digest her words and figure how I would finance my trip. *Oh yeah, the voucher.* "I'll be there."

The next day at the service counter, I handed the voucher to the attendant.

"I'm going to Dallas, Texas from the 8th to the 12th. How much will that be?"

"Well, on such short notice, it will be quite a bit more than this voucher."

"Gosh, my grandpa died yesterday. I don't have cash to cover that."

"Oh, if it's for a family member's funeral, then we discount it generously. Let me see how much extra you would owe. OK, you'll only owe $31.35 for tax."

"Great."

"Oh, I forgot—we don't charge tax in this type circumstance, so you don't owe anything."

"You mean the voucher is the exact amount of the ticket?"

"That's right, nothing owed and nothing back."

When I arrived in Texas, I told Grandma how my unexpected flight was a special journey. It was a praise report of God's faithfulness, and it lifted our spirits.

Yes, we grieved, knowing we would not see my grandfather again in this life, but we also rejoiced that we will see him in heaven. I was happily relieved that before Grandpa left, I had told him that I would one day see him in Heaven.

Spider Spit

By Mark L. Hoffman
Lititz, Pennsylvania, United States

I am a writer. I wrote my first poem at the age of 10 and my first short story before I turned 13, and I haven't stopped rhyming or telling tales since. Some people struggle to put one word in front of the other, while others are as nimble and as graceful with their words as Fred Astaire was with his feet. I always believed I was the latter, though sometimes my efforts to carve out a writing career had all the grace of Jerry Lewis.

Many people believed in me, but they also saw my undisciplined side and encouraged me to channel my writing into a more structured position. It's OK to write for a living, as long as you are sure that you are earning a living, they said. Not only do rejection slips not put food on the table, but they are hard on the digestive system as well, they reminded me. I listened to them and put much of my creative side on the shelf to help pay the bills.

I became a public relations professional—a PR man. I was still a wordsmith, I told myself. I was stringing words together to tell a story...and, oh, the stories I told. Not my story of course, but a story nevertheless.

Yes, putting words together to generate publicity sure paid the bills, but it wasn't the same. A writer I was, but not a happy one.

I was a well fed, but discontented scribbler who dreamed of writing a novel—not necessarily the "great American novel," but perhaps a pretty darn good one. Heck, I was willing to settle for a short story or a nice little vignette, as long as it was published with my name attached to it.

My wife encouraged me to write whenever I had free time. Magazines published my non-fiction articles. But still the book lay waiting. Not enough free time, I told myself, family, and friends. And, then *it* happened. My prayers were answered, sort of.

I lost my job. Oh, I hadn't planned to lose my job nor done anything intentional to prompt dismissal. One morning, I woke up and went to work like normal and then came home early—for good.

Watch out for what you pray for. Just when you're thinking that God is not paying attention, He provides you with in-your-face convincing proof that He was listening all along. It was you that ignored things, not Him. Here I was—46 years old and fired, but I wasn't scared. I felt—no, I knew—this was part of God's plan.

That evening, our pastor prayed with my wife and me. The next morning, the two of us knelt at the end of our bed and prayed together for peace of mind and guidance.

After she left for work, I went to a nearby park for a long walk. It was foggy morning. The white, pale mist hung low to the ground, and I could see my hand in front of my face, but not much further. I walked along slowly, presumably alone, in the fog. The mist began breaking up, but ever so slowly. The park walk was a two-mile loop—one mile in and one mile out.

As I walked, I thought about writing. With each footfall, a sentence or two fell into shape. All of a sudden, I stopped writing in my head, and started praying with my heart. I asked God the question that was heavy on the hearts of my wife and I: *Was now the time for the real writing to begin?* I reminded myself and God of my hopes and dreams. I asked God for His guidance. I asked Jesus to be my partner—my pen pal, if you will.

As I made the turn and began the one-mile return loop, the sun popped up, and the fog melted away. Not only could I see where I had been, but I could finally see where I was going. I started to appreciate God's sense of humor. But He had far more in store than just one little cliché. The Creator of the Universe had done me one better.

On the way back, I was treated to the sight of three outrageously complex and wonderfully crafted, beautiful spider webs. I hadn't seen them on my way into the park because of the fog, but the parting mists had revealed an unparalleled gallery of "arachnid art." The dew and misty remnants hung heavily on the silken threads, making them shine like strands of silver and diamonds. The intricate patterns were almost intoxicating—concentric circles, like ripples on a pond, glistened and sparkled in the bright early morning sun. The creativity of those tiny little creatures was enchanting and enthralling—spellbinding. I stared transfixed at the webs.

Then I started to cry. I was so humbled. This wasn't just a spider web. God was clearly speaking to me.

Oh, I take that back—God wasn't speaking, He was shouting.

Here's what my heart heard God say as I stared at the webs: "If these little spiders with brains no bigger than a mustard seed can weave spider spit to create incredible works of art, just imagine, Mark, what you and I can do together with words on a piece of paper!"

There was no ignoring the signs. I not only took them to heart, but I put them into practice, as well. I went home and started to write. Not only was the book a good idea, it was now—as far as I was concerned—God's idea. And, God's ideas beat good ideas any day. That alone will ensure its success.

The book is coming along nicely. I have found additional work with a magazine and newspaper, and *Reader's Digest* has asked permission to reprint an earlier story. But, to tell the truth, nothing I have written so far is as majestic as those spider webs. Then again, I'm not using spider spit.

But, with Jesus as my pen pal, God as my writing coach, and my wife as my editor, all things are possible.

Twice Blessed

By P. Jeanne Davis
Philadelphia, Pennsylvania, United States

It was an overcast spring morning in 1990 when my husband, John, and I were awakened by that life-altering telephone call at 6:00 a.m.

"It's a boy!"

Immediately we knew this was the voice of the birth grandmother of the child that was soon to be ours.

"He is beautiful," she continued.

Although it was a dreary and wet morning, we took little notice—for us the sun had broken through the clouds. My husband and I couldn't get to the hospital quickly enough. I was first to hold him.

You're meant to be my son, I thought as I picked him up in my arms. He was beautiful.

We had waited for this moment for a long time. Now, after many conversations over the telephone, we met the young woman who was giving him to us to be his parents. We were so grateful to God, to our son's birth mother, and to all involved in making this possible. John and I could bring our baby home in three days.

The arrival of a child into our home for the first time, when we were in our mid-40's, is remarkable and clearly due to divine orchestration.

******

During the early years of our marriage, we realized the chance of a pregnancy was small due to my age. This situation was further complicated by endometriosis—a chronic condition thought to be responsible for my infertility.

By my early 40's, I had had several surgeries to bring physical relief, but had little hope of having children. Now my age was increasingly becoming a factor.

"It's not utterly impossible, but it's extremely improbable you'll become pregnant," I was informed by my gynecologist.

"You might wish to consider an adoption," she suggested with genuine interest. She gave us all the information on an upcoming adoption seminar, and we attended.

At first, John and I weren't certain this was what we wanted to do.

Eventually, we became very enthusiastic about this way of creating our family. Since we were well above the age limit for an agency adoption, we retained an attorney who specialized in private independent adoptions. Because I worked in a hospital and had many contacts, I did much networking there. When telling others about our desire to adopt, I found, to my surprise, that I was far less timid than I had expected.

One and a half years elapsed with no real adoption prospects. Nevertheless, we were still determined, hopeful, and kept getting the word out, always relying on God's promise: *"In all your ways acknowledge Him, and He will make your paths straight."* Proverbs 3:6

I clearly recall the afternoon I returned home and, on an impulse, attempted to contact the doctor who had first suggested adoption. Of course, I hoped she might be of further help.

When I was told she had relocated and now practiced in another part of our state, even this didn't discourage me. I was amazed by my determination.

"What's her new number?" I asked. The desire to have a family was now intense. And having come this far, I was unwilling to stop now. I promptly dialed her new number and was informed she was with a new patient. I left my name and telephone number.

When she returned my call, my former gynecologist had no clue as to the reason for the contact, but she did remember us.

I explained and assured her that we'd completed all the requirements for a private adoption. She promised to let us know if she could be of further assistance to us. Again, we had established another possible source for an independent adoption.

When will we be successful? we wondered.

Our answer was to come just 10 days later when a separate telephone line we had reserved for adoption rang. We received very few calls on this line. I silently prayed as I answered the telephone.

"Jeanne, I have a baby for you." Our physician-friend was calling again from her home.

I was too excited to say anything. My heart jumped.

She went on to explain. "The very afternoon you called my office, a young girl and her mother had arrived. Tests taken then later showed she was pregnant," she continued. "The birth mother felt she would be unable to give her baby a good life. In the days that followed her initial appointment, she made the decision to find a Bible believing home for her child. After I told her about you, she decided she would like you to raise this child."

My physician-friend said the timing of my call that day and this office visit for a pregnancy test was a "remarkable coincidence."

But was it "God's hand," or was it the long arm of coincidence?

I truly felt this wasn't just merely a quirky chance happening. God was truly directing my path when I made that call.

And we could provide for this child exactly what his birth mother wanted—a loving, nurturing home for a much wanted baby. Her request was, "Give him lots of love."

With this child, my husband and I now felt our family was complete. We were a happy couple caring for our first little one.

Yet, one year after the birth of John, we were to discover that with God nothing is impossible—that He has His own perfect timing for all events in our lives.

For several weeks in the spring of 1991, I insisted I must have the flu. But why did it last so long? Occasionally, I considered the possibility that I might be pregnant. But could it really be possible? I was soon to be 48 years old and had been told I would most likely never experience a pregnancy.

"I think I might be pregnant," I told my husband. Yet even as I said this, I found it hard to believe.

Then: "Your pregnancy test is positive!" said my primary care physician with obvious excitement in her voice.

After the initial surprise and joy, I couldn't help but wonder, *How will I cope with two babies at my age? Will the baby be healthy?*

My pregnancy went smoothly except that the baby was in breech position until delivery. Joshua was a full term baby, born c-section.

"This is truly a miracle baby!" my obstetrician exclaimed when she entered my hospital room. "One for the records, for sure. Just your age alone makes it extraordinary."

Eventually I wrote to the gynecologist who had helped with our adoption. I wanted to inform her of the new addition. A few months later, while talking with her over the telephone, it became apparent she had misunderstood my letter when she said, "You've adopted another child."

It took some moments to convince her I had given birth.

"I can't believe it! What a wonderful surprise!" was her stunned reaction.

Today, both of our boys are in elementary school, and they keep their parents very busy. I enjoy staying at home to care for my family. When some days are rough and I feel the demands of childrearing, I remember how God responded to the desire of our hearts in a special way.

Although I came to motherhood very late in life, I feel as if I've recaptured those years while deepening my faith in God.

The Faith of a Father

By Pamela Troeppl-Kinnaird
Shoreline, Washington, United States

I've given birth to four extraordinary children. Of course, the fact that they are mine in no way makes my opinion biased, does it? Each of their births was unique, and each child brought their own little personality into our world, expanding our circle of love. Each birth was a leap of faith for my family, and each experience was an exercise in love. But my fourth baby was a one-in-a-million baby—literally.

Throughout my pregnancy with Ashley, I had a feeling that something wasn't quite as it should be. The still, small voice that whispers to your heart fervently whispered to mine and told me that this child was special. Through the years, I've learned to listen to that voice. It brought me to my husband of 15 years, it has taught me right from wrong, and I know that it comes from the Lord. By listening to the whisperings of the Holy Spirit, I have been blessed in many ways. When I fail to listen, my life seems to go awry.

This time, I was being told in my mind and in my heart that something was wrong with the tiny angel I carried within me. This time I listened.

I was seven months into a fairly uneventful pregnancy, when I suddenly knew in my heart that something wasn't right. Whatever was wrong, it was serious. Not knowing what *it* was exactly, but with the whisperings of the Spirit, a mother's intuition, and an increasing sense of apprehension, I phoned my doctor. I told her that I felt something was wrong with my baby, and she told me to come right in.

As I lay on the examining table having an ultrasound, I asked the doctor if a baby could have a seizure in the womb. She informed me that, yes, it probably could happen, but it would be rare. Well, if there was something rare and unusual, it was going to happen to me, so I told her that I believed my little girl had suffered a seizure. Thankfully, she knew me enough to trust my instincts. I'd felt a strange movement in my womb two days previously and then had felt nothing since—nothing but dread as the Spirit whispered to my heart that my child was in danger.

After ascertaining that my baby had a heartbeat, my doctor sent me over to the hospital for more tests. I knew all about these tests, having suffered two miscarriages and severe complications during my pregnancy with my third child.

Clutching the hand of my sweet husband, I silently prayed that my baby would be all right.

Even to my untrained eye, I could tell that there was something seriously wrong during the ultrasound exam. My infant appeared to be lifeless, floating in the amniotic fluid. There was no movement whatsoever. At one point, the ultrasound technician pressed the wand more fiercely into my abdomen, and I heard her whisper under her breath, "Oh baby, please move a little." She never did. Through my tears, I prayed even harder for the life of my child.

As I was wheeled back down to the maternity ward, the OB on call came running out from behind the nurses' desk yelling, "Your baby is dying, and we don't know why! You're going back up so I can see the test for myself."

Sobbing, I was quickly whisked back up to the examining room where the lengthy exam was repeated.

While I was being examined, my sister called the hospital, and my husband told her to call my parents and to come right away. They arrived in record time to find me back in my room, standing up and walking around. I'd been told that they needed to do a crash c-section on me to save my baby's life. Since I knew that I would be in bed for quite a while after this operation, I wanted to walk around as long as possible. It also helped calm my nerves a bit. My parents finally prevailed upon me to return to my bed. What I hadn't been told them was that this emergency operation would also put my life at risk, as well, and my family was more than a little concerned.

My mother cried, and my father suggested that I have a priesthood blessing. I'd never anticipated the words of a blessing more than I did that afternoon in that hospital room.

My sister closed my hospital room door and pulled the privacy curtain around my bed. My husband anointed me, and my father placed his hands on my head and gave the blessing, pausing several times as the Spirit gave him the words to pronounce. He told me that the Lord knew what I was going through and that my baby would be born alive and would live. He said that this child would be a blessing unto our entire family.

The room seemed to be filled with the spirit of the Lord, and we were overcome with gratitude, knowing that the Lord was aware of the yearnings of our hearts for this tiny infant that I carried.

As they wheeled me into the operating room, my sister gave me one last hug, and I whispered in her ear that if my little girl didn't make it, to hold her for me and to tell her that her mommy loved her. I knew I would be unconscious and unable to know what had occurred for several hours. Sobbing, she held onto me and promised that she would do as I'd asked.

Then my father leaned over me, looked deeply into my eyes, and said, "Honey, didn't you listen to the blessing? All will be well. I promise you that everything will be all right."

I felt at peace.

In the three years since Ashley's premature birth, Dad has delighted in asking me over and over again, "You didn't believe me, did you? I told you she would live." And he was right.

Ashley had suffered more than just a seizure in the womb; she'd had a stroke. The doctors told us that her prognosis was unknown. She might not walk, she might not talk, and she might not have a normal life.

They didn't take into account the power of a priesthood blessing and the faith of my father.

Now Ashley walks with the aid of a brace. At three years of age, she has the vocabulary an eight year-old might envy, and she has indeed been a blessing to our entire family. She's also a living, breathing testimony to all who see her of the importance of listening to the still small voice of the Holy Spirit and what a father's faith can do with the power of the priesthood.

Heartbeat

By Dawn M. Coder
Palm Harbor, Florida, United States

June 14, 1998
    I found out I was pregnant on this day. I had been with the same man for a couple of years on and off, and when I discovered that I was pregnant with his child, I did not know what to do. We had used birth control, and I had been told by two different surgeons that I could not get pregnant due to severe endometriosis. So when I saw the test stick had two lines instead of one, I almost passed out.

    My endometriosis specialist verified that I was pregnant, and he suggested I make an appointment with my neurologist as soon as possible. I have a neurologist, because I also have epilepsy, and I am on massive amounts of an anti-convulsant medication called Neurontin to keep my seizures under control. I knew that this could not be good for my baby. I was scared, and he got me into the office the same day I called.

    When I told him I was pregnant, the comment I got from this usually very nice, conscientious man went something like this: "What do you mean, you're pregnant? Do you know what this means? Do you realize you have a seizure disorder? Do you realize you cannot stop taking your medication, and if you decide to go through with this, you are putting your own life at risk? You have to get an abortion to save your own life!"

    Imagine how I reacted to that. I sat there in silence. My doctor told me not to come back if I didn't want to listen to him.

He stated he did not know what kind of effects Neurontin might have on a baby, but he did make it clear that pregnancy could induce more seizures because of how fast the hormones change—and since I was prone to having seizures around my menstrual cycle to begin with, he was more afraid for me—that this could cause them to generalize. (I have complex-partial seizures, meaning they are not the grand mal seizures that people think of when they hear the word "epilepsy." However, these types of seizures can go into secondary generalized, meaning that if they are out of control, I could have a grand mal. Thankfully, I have never had one.)

What was I to do? I came home crying my heart out. As much as I did not want a child at that point in my life, I didn't think I could bring myself to get an abortion. I did, however, make an appointment with a clinic about an hour south of here, and with a heavy heart, I told them that I would be coming alone. They set it up for a week from the day I made the call.

In the meantime, I did research on the Internet. I spent hours and hours and hours online researching women with epilepsy and pregnancy, and Neurontin and the effects of the drug on the unborn baby.

What I found did not make me feel any better. It seemed that my neurologist was right. There was not enough research done on Neurontin to determine if it would cause birth defects, brain abnormalities, spina bifida, or anything else. It was too new of a drug to determine anything—including long-term effects on the people taking it.

I decided that I had no choice but to get an abortion. I told only two of my closest friends and the father that I was going to do this, and they all said they would support my decision.

Then something changed my mind. One thing made me decide to take my own life and my baby's life in my hands. It was a sign from God.

The nine-week-old fetus in my abdomen had a heart-beat.

That is what changed my mind.

This child that I was never supposed to be able to have, this child that was moving and growing inside of me, had a heart that was working. It was beating. It was alive. What right did I have to take that life? After all, isn't a mother supposed to put her child's life first?

I decided I would continue to take the drug. I would take my chances. I would, for the first time in my life, take a life-threatening risk—all because I had another life inside that was depending on me. How could I not take the chance?

I was scared, sure. I was afraid—literally—for my life. I made another two appointments: one with my neurologist, who told me that I was no longer a patient of his; and one with my endometriosis specialist, who congratulated me on my bravery and promised me that he would take care of me and my baby by setting me up with the area's best high-risk pregnancy specialist.

That day, when I was nine weeks along, I saw my baby's heartbeat for the first time, and I cried. The technician said it was highly unusual to see the fetal heart on an ultrasound so early in the pregnancy and that it was a miracle. She was as shocked as I was.

But there it was, and I knew deep down I had made the right decision.

February 11, 1999
This is the day my son was born. After a long, painful, illness-filled but seizure-free pregnancy, I gave birth to a healthy 7-pound, 3-ounce baby boy. He has no defects, and he is beautiful.

He is now three years old, and I cannot imagine my life without him. He's perfect, and I never stopped taking my medicine throughout the pregnancy. As rough as the pregnancy was, I will never let a doctor try and talk me into having an abortion again. I know now that God helped me make the right choices, and if I had to do it all over again, I surely would. Many times.

I thank God every day when I look at my beautiful Daniel. I am still amazed that after being told by two surgeons I could not get pregnant, and after using birth control, I still gave birth to a beautiful, healthy baby boy against all odds.

My Godsend

By Avis McGriff Rasmussen
Riverside, California, United States

Dennis and I met for the first time in January 1993. We were married in June 1995 and have been together for seven years. Ours is a love story of pure design.

In 1986, Dennis had moved from the midwestern United States to attend a law school in Southern California. He graduated, began his new career as an attorney, and later began volunteering with the Alumni Association. Eventually, he initiated a campaign for a new scholarship fund to assist the law students.

While living in Northern California, I was encouraged by some close friends to attend the same law school. I applied and was accepted in April 1992. Shortly after being accepted to law school, however, I learned that I had a serious illness. My doctor discovered I had several tumors, and since there were no medical specialists in Northern California practicing the latest technology in dealing with my illness, my doctor suggested that I seek help while in Southern California.

I began law school in August 1992, somewhat in denial of my illness. By November 1992, I had settled in to my study and work routines, but my illness escalated. It became necessary to shorten my work hours. I also spoke with the college dean about discontinuing law school. Thankfully, he encouraged me to pray about completing the first class term. My new doctor also agreed that I should be able to continue with my studies. A few weeks after speaking with the dean, one of the law school alum distributed scholarship notices in the first year law classes.

Since I did not know if I would complete the whole year of school, I was hesitant to compete for the scholarship. Finally, my sister suggested that I really had nothing to lose. When I slid my application under the university registrar's office door late one evening in December 1992, I had no idea of the significance of that one small act. Looking back, I can clearly see that God was directing Dennis and I to each other.

In January 1993, the scholarship selection committee contacted all of the scholarship candidates, and my name was on that wonderful list! When I met with the committee, Dennis was sitting across the table with the other interviewers. I received one of the scholarships and was invited to take a picture with Dennis who handed me my check.

During March 1993, I finally had to leave school to deal with my illness. I had surgery and was back on my feet in time to complete the first year final exams in May. While resting from surgery, I decided to take some time away from school after finals. This was a difficult decision because school was very important to me.

I also spent a lot of time in prayer about my future, in or out of school. There is something about dealing with serious illness that reshapes one's thinking about the important things in life. I came to a crossroads in my life. I could have gone in any direction and ended up in a good place, but God seemed to be nudging me to consider marriage. Since I had never seriously thought about being married, I found this nudging a bit odd.

Although I was still contemplating the direction for my life, I wanted to see where God's nudging would lead. The answer came in a way that caught me completely by surprise. I was given a hint of the answer in December 1993 when I attended a Christmas party hosted in the home of the dean of the law school.

Yes, you guessed it. Dennis was also at the party. We had not spoken in nearly a year, and we only spoke in passing at the party. But as we later confirmed with each other, during our brief talk that night, there was a mutual knowing in our spirits that our meeting was intentional.

The answer to God's nudge was finally revealed to me in January 1994 when Dennis called to ask me to have a "business" lunch with him to discuss school events. After our chat at the party, I was running scared and tried to avoid his advances. He was persistent, however, and kept asking me out. Well, he not only convinced me to have lunch with him, but he paid for the meal. I left the restaurant bewildered from the obvious amiable connection I felt with Dennis. I certainly did not like having allowed him to pay for my lunch when we were only having a "business" lunch. I wondered what God was doing with my life by introducing me to this man.

However, before I could fully digest the meaning of Dennis's advances and deal with my fears about marriage, he called me to ask me out to dinner. Although I had decided to back out of any future relations with him, I felt that nudge from God again, during the telephone call, to listen to Dennis and not hurt him. I was in awe of God's timing for providing me with a potential husband, but a bit upset that I was being nudged to consider Dennis. I thought we would have problems since Dennis is Caucasian and I am African American. Frankly, I did not know how my family would accept him or if his would want me. And Dennis also shared his concerns about our being from different backgrounds and family acceptance.

As only God could design, Dennis and I decided to consider becoming closer and we asked our friends to pray for us. When we finally moved past our initial inhibitions, we found that we were more concerned about what our friends and family members would think about our relationship than they were. All of our friends immediately embraced our dating, and many of them attended our wedding. Our family members did caution us, but, in the end, they were very delighted that we had decided to date and later marry. In fact, Dennis even asked my dad for my hand in marriage, which was a great honor to my father and me. He even went a step further and asked my mom, and other members of my family if they would accept him into the family. He made me very proud of him.

Dennis and I have been married for seven years. Together, we have a son, David, a blessing I had believed would not be possible due to my illness. Dennis and David have brought a lot of happiness to my life. They have taught me how to stop and smell the roses along life's busy pathways. I do not know where God is leading me from here, but I am certainly glad that I followed the nudges several years ago that brought me to the road leading to marriage and motherhood.

Forget Me Knots

By Helen Kay Polaski
Milan, Michigan, United States

Even as a young girl, I knew I would write a book some day. Don't ask me how or why I knew this—I just did. My goal was to capture my family forever on hundreds of sheets of paper. It was a big goal. Imagine trying to contain 11 sisters, 4 brothers, your mom and dad, and aunts and uncles forever in a timeless volume.

Of course, no one believed me. Looking back, I suppose I can't blame them. After all, what did I know about writing? The most I could say for myself was that I had a voracious appetite for books. I read anything I could get my hands on.

Still, I knew I would be an author. I just knew. It wasn't an idea, nor was it a thought, really. It was more a statement that tickled its way through my mind from time to time, reinforcing my need to devote more and more time to scribbling inside a notebook.

A book would ensure I never forgot my roots, and someday the world would enjoy reading about my families' antics. Never did it cross my mind that everyone else might not be interested in reading stories about my family, and I'm glad to say it did not. Had that thought penetrated, I might have stopped writing before I had truly begun. So once again, I thank God for the insistent idea that I would be a writer. It was a gentle reinforcement, a nudge that kept me going in the right direction.

From the time I was big enough to drag around a Big Chief tablet, I did. Perhaps that was why my father, who had a nickname for each of his children, called me Big Chief. Who knows? What I do know is that when I had a tablet in my hands, nothing could sway me from my mission.

My stories grew from crayon scribbles to sentences and paragraphs that began to make sense.

I believe I actually had some writing talent, but no one in my community or school encouraged me to pursue my dream. My high school counselor said I should take classes that might land me a secretarial job, but that I should also realize I might end up working as a waitress or a cleaning lady. College was never suggested. Writing—and my one other career aspiration at the time—modeling—were both swept under the rug.

In fact, when I graduated from high school in 1974, I had already exceeded the expectations of our community in doing that. It seems that in coming from a family of 16 children, graduating was about the biggest thing they expected any of us to accomplish…ever.

After graduation, I left home and followed the plan already mapped out for me—I got a job as a secretary. But I couldn't keep myself from following my heart. In my spare time, I filled notebook after notebook with stories and poetry.

I married in 1976, quit my secretarial job, and had three children. When I wasn't awake in the middle of the night tending to a child, I was up writing down the things that were floating around in my head, preventing me from getting a full night's rest. I thank God for the insight to keep a tablet—alas, no longer a Big Chief—at my bedside. Once the ideas, poems, or stories were committed to paper, sleep came easily.

Urged on by a strong feeling that I was going to be somebody in this lifetime, I continued writing. I enrolled in a writing class and learned the correct way to write children's stories. Then I learned how to write Girl Scout features and began jotting down my daughters' adventures. I shoved them under the door at *The Milan News* and was ecstatic when I read my work in the feature section of the newspaper every week.

But that was not enough. I wanted to write stories about my own childhood.

When my youngest was only a year old, I joined the local newspaper staff and quickly became editor and photographer as well as reporter and cleaning lady. For the next 17 years, I wrote. Part of my dream had come true. I was writing, but it was about everyone else's life. And though I was happy, the voice in my head urging me to write that book was just as insistent as it had been in years past. I knew I needed to get my childhood stories between the pages of a book. Finally, at the suggestion of my husband, I quit the paper and turned my thoughts inward.

Within two years, I had numerous articles printed online and nearly a dozen short stories accepted in print books. I decided it was time to shift into high gear.

To be an author of a book, one has to write a book. So I did. It was a romance novel, and it wasn't bad, but it didn't give me the sense of accomplishment I sought. The voice whispered in my ear again and reminded me that I wanted to write about childhood, not romance.

One day, it came to me. I would put together an anthology of childhood stories from around the world. The title was easy. Forget-me-nots had always been a favorite flower, especially after my mother and I dug up English daisies in her lawn one afternoon for me to take home, and the next year forget-me-nots grew in their place—both in my flowerbed and in her lawn. We teased that it was a sign sent to the both of us so we would not forget one another. It was meant as a joke—nothing more—but when my mother passed away several years later, I realized it for the sign it was. Every time I see forget-me-nots, I am reminded of Mom's beautiful smile and infectious laugh.

So I titled my book, *Forget Me Knots...from the Front Porch*. (At the suggestion of a friend, I added the "K" to the word "nots." Since memories are the knots that bind us to our childhood, the play on words seemed to fit.)

One evening toward midnight, as my family slept, I sat in my office alone, the room illuminated only by the light from my computer screen, and painstakingly copied and pasted information about my proposed book into as many search engines and newsletters as I could find. But even as I sat there working hard on this project and was sure the book would eventually come to pass, I was plagued with doubt. Would my book sell? Would anyone other than me and those authors who had added their personal childhood stories want a copy of the book? What if this was nothing more than a time-consuming, expensive venture on my part?

An overwhelming sense of dread flowed through me, and I stopped typing. I slumped back in my chair as anxiety twisted my stomach. *Oh, God, what if no one wanted to read it?*

Suddenly, the scent of powdered talc crept into the room. My eyes grew wide, and I tentatively sniffed again. Bath talc...no doubt about it. The same kind Mom always wore.

My eyes filled with tears as I realized she was in the room with me, supporting me as she had always done.

With a trembling smile, I whispered, "Hey, Mom..." and drew one last breath filled with her scent. Then she was gone, her mission accomplished.

I was immediately convinced God had sent her to let me know I was on the right track.

As soon as I got my website up and running, I started letting friends in on what I was doing. When the Editor in Chief of Obadiah Press, Tina Miller, a woman I had met earlier in the year, told me she and her partner had opened a Christian publishing house and they were interested in publishing my book, I was elated. It felt right.

But then, as the days dragged into weeks and then months, I started to feel anxious again. There is so much to do to publish a book!

As a Roman Catholic, I have always taken comfort in the rosary and often turned to holding and praying the rosary in times of stress in my life. During this time, I started going to bed with a rosary, praying that all would work out in God's perfect timing.

About that same time, I opened the mail one day to find a new brochure from a missionary I had ordered merchandise from in the past. As I opened the envelope, I had to sit down. There on the page was a beautiful silver rosary with deep blue beads and a locket in the center. Across the top of the page were the words: "The Forget-Me-Not rosary." I sniffed back tears, took a deep breath, then reached for my checkbook and ordered one for me and one for my sister, Melissa Szymanski, who was doing the cover art for my book. Here was another nudge that I was on the right track.

The rosaries arrived two weeks later, and the note attached said they had already been blessed. I guess God figured I needed this particular rosary in my hands ASAP. I whispered, "Thank You, Lord," and tucked the rosary into my pocket.

By this time, things were really coming together. The book was at the publisher for final edits, all galleys had been approved, and all but three author contracts were in my hands. So when my husband suggested we travel to northern Michigan and rent a cottage on Nettie Bay—near our old stompin' grounds—for the weekend, I jumped at the chance.

By mid-October, flowers have long since stopped blooming and several frosts have painted the trees to brilliant orange, red, and yellow. This would be the perfect get-away—one the whole family would appreciate.

Despite some fog, we weren't disappointed. The view was gorgeous, and the weekend was filled with fun activities for our entire family. Still, that familiar old anxiety was with me, and though I had been fighting it all weekend, I was losing the battle. Who was I that people would buy my book? What made me think I could do this?

As my anxiety heightened, I glanced outside and noticed the sun had broken through the clouds. A bright patch of sunlight on the far side of the lake illuminating the autumn colors seemed to call out to me, and since anything was better than worrying about things I could not control, I quickly slipped on my shoes and walked down to the water for a diversion.

As I stepped onto the dock, a sense of peace flowed through me. I walked to the end of the dock and looked at all of God's beauty surrounding me, and I was in awe. With all of this beauty, how did I fit into God's plan?

Feeling very small and insignificant, I drew a deep breath and turned around to face the shore. What I saw next caused my vision to blur. My knees gave way, and I nearly sat down on the dock, the revelation was so poignant.

Forget-me-nots lined the beach. Though out of season, the blue flowers bobbed gently in the stiff autumn breeze as if they knew their mission and were proud to have accomplished it.

Giddy with relief and restored confidence, I walked back to the cabin on unsteady legs and once again whispered, "Thank You, Lord."

Since that moment, whenever I feel anxiety threatening to overwhelm me, I think of Mom and forget-me-nots and am reminded that I am part of the big picture. Though I often feel small and insignificant, I know that I am important to God—and so are my dreams. Whenever I begin to doubt myself, He always nudges me in the right direction.

5

Are You Listening to Him?

God's voice thunders in marvelous ways;
he does great things beyond our understanding.
—Job 37:5

Never Say Never

By Cathy Laska
Wausau, Wisconsin, USA

"Are you kidding?" I said to the gentleman from a mission organization at the other end of the phone. "I would *never* go to Africa—too many poisonous snakes, too hot, and just a dangerous place to be!"

Politely, the gentleman responded, "It's safest to be in the Lord's hands if that's where He wants you."

"Not me—*never*! But thank you for the information," I replied as I hung up the phone.

By this time, I must have researched hundreds of organizations to figure out where I wanted to go and what I really wanted to do. Would the missions be short term or full? Why were doors closing to Scotland, England, and Romania only weeks after they opened?

Ah, yes, Romania—a place that intrigued me—took hold of me! My mind visualized pictures of Romania, culturally different and full of the beautiful countryside. How could I not want to go there?

It sounded like a simple feat. I would just go there and love up on orphaned children. I had heard organizations were in need of volunteers. My "heels dug in" and my mind determined, I set my goal to go in one year.

It's only been about four years since I spoke to the gentleman about Africa, so what's one more year to wait? God would work it out. My motives and heart were in the right place. My heart became more attached, my thoughts deeper, and my spirit more excited with every child that caught my eye.

Then, one hot day in July, it happened. Returning home from a long day at work, I took in the smell of the fresh cut grass that surrounded my Atlanta complex. As I opened the door to my apartment, like I did every summer evening after work, my thoughts moved forward to getting my bathing suit on and enjoying the sparkling cool water of the complex pool.

Yet, this time when I passed through my living room, I felt a deep, strong urge inside to turn on the black box with the picture screen. As I turned the television on, I saw an anchorman for the World News standing amidst several sun-toned children with small bodies and big eyes at an HIV orphanage in Karen, Kenya, just outside Nairobi. Obviously touched by what he saw, a plea for volunteers to come and stay for any length of time came out of his crackling voice.

The moment I heard the need and saw the children, my eyes welled up with uncontrollable tears that ran down my face. I lifted my head toward the ceiling, my eyes seeing beyond and above to a Heavenly Father. *Lord, is this really where You want me to go? Are You sure it's Africa?* Certain of what I had just heard and seen, I could not blot out the memory of the little faces that tugged at my heartstrings during such a short lapse of time.

Lord, if this is really what You want me to do, I'm scared, but I'll do it. Please confirm this and provide all my needs. When do I go? How long do I stay?

This was July, going into August. Was it possible that God wanted me to go in October when my summer job ended? It would be autumn here, yet the beginning of summer in Africa—such little time to prepare.

I once thought my faith had been fairly strong, but now I became a Doubting Thomas. *God, I need someone to lease this apartment for those three months. Who could I trust living in my home with all my belongings?*

I needed to get my immunizations. *What about my passport, airline ticket, and money for the trip? Are You sure You can handle this, God? Are You sure I am to go?* Like Gideon in the Old Testament, I lay down a fleece before the Lord.

He wrote my support letter to my church, family, and friends. I even tried to sabotage the trip by sending the letter out late.

Now 10 weeks before I was to go, I waited anxiously, curious to see how the Lord would come through on this. It could only be a miracle waiting to happen in a big God way.

As the days passed by and I took the first step of faith by getting my shots, I saw God working in miraculous ways. Day after day, I stepped out with baby steps of faith, and day after day, God provided.

Nearly three weeks later, the Lord directed me to a young woman in our church who needed a place to stay for the exact time I was to be gone and could only afford a certain amount— the exact amount I had in mind for rent.

Days later, I received checks in the mail that would cover my passport and immunizations with a few dollars left over. Another week went by, and checks accumulated to equal my airfare. Necessities were met, day after day. With two weeks left, all my financial needs were met and ticket and passport enroute.

There was one more matter to conquer though. I was deathly afraid of snakes, and Africa had the crude and hot environment vipers survive in. What if I met up with one? What about the big mosquitoes that carried malaria? Even my doctor had told me I was signing my own death warrant.

A pastor friend within the church encouraged me to go forward and said that it was up to God to close the doors or keep them open as He pleased.

Well, God never shut the door, and before I knew it, I stepped off a large jet into a blazing heat of 100-degree weather. The heat waves surrounded me as I felt my mouth become parched. Beads of sweat seeped through my clothing, dripping onto the extremely dry, flat terrain of Kenya. The only thing visible at this distance was complete and utter bareness.

My mind reverted back to my Atlanta complex and the sweet smelling aroma of the magnolia trees in full bloom. Oh, how I missed the crisp fresh air and the sparkling cool water of the complex pool!

I was as close to the equator as I could possibly get, and I couldn't turn back. It was too late. I had no idea what God might have in store for me, but I knew He had lessons for me to learn, lessons I could only learn through experience.

And I had just passed one of the first and probably most valuable: *Never say never!*

Out of the Valley

By Nanette Snipes
Buford, Georgia, United States

Christmas of 1974 brought me to my knees as I came to grips with my recent divorce. The year before, during a terror-filled weekend, my husband of 11 years had threatened me with a loaded gun.

I recall sitting on the edge of the bed watching him throw his clothes into an open suitcase. The air between us crackled with electricity, and I struggled to control my breathing. I had asked for a separation because his all-nighters had finally taken a toll on me. Months of threats had left me few options. His eyes burned with rage, and he decided he would be the one to leave.

The dream I'd had the week before simmered in the back of my mind. In the dream, my husband had been angry as he pointed a gun at my midsection. I remember screaming. He kept shouting at me to "Shut up!" but I continued to scream. Shots rang out, and clutching my stomach, I fell to the floor. In the dream, I knew I was dying.

I was jolted back to the present as he slammed his shirts into the suitcase. He stopped abruptly. A change came over him, and he said, "I'm not leaving, and if you leave me, I'll just have to kill you." With slow deliberation, he closed and locked both bedroom doors and each window, then walked into the large closet. I watched in disbelief as he reached for the .38 magnum and pulled it down. He clutched a boxful of shells with the other hand. Slowly he turned toward me, his eyes glazed and distant. I heard each bullet click into place as he loaded the chambers, and I measured my life with each click. I could feel my dream repeating itself, and at once, I knew the warning had come from God.

I had never known real fear until that day when my husband thrust the gun in my face. At first, I screamed hysterically, then recalled the dream where he shouted, "Shut up!" Since I knew he was agitated, I whispered a silent prayer. "Lord, I want to live. I want to see my children grow up. Please help me."

I felt I was out of time, and I closed my eyes ready to breathe my last. In that short space of time, it was as though God spoke out loud. *Tell him you love him.* I didn't hesitate. I obeyed what the Lord said.

I did love my husband, so it wasn't hard to say. I knew, though, that I would never be able to live with him again. I spoke the words.

He trembled, then lowered the gun. I didn't know how close I'd really come to dying that day until later.

While sitting side by side on the bed, he talked about the event. I shuddered inwardly. While the violence was not new, I had no idea just how detailed his plan was. As a result of the escalating violence, I made plans to leave.

That long weekend, after the gun ordeal, my husband wouldn't let me out of his sight for even a minute. I felt like a prisoner in my own home. He made sure we were inseparable, but mentally and spiritually, we were far apart.

Making sure everything appeared normal that gray Monday morning, I left for work with my two boys, ages four and seven. I even dropped them off at daycare. As I watched the boys enter the building, I wept. I felt so lost and alone. The only thing I could cling to was a Psalm I memorized in Vacation Bible School—particularly, the part that said, "...Even though I walk through the valley of the shadow of death, I will fear no evil, for you are with me…"

For my sanity and our safety, we had to leave. But I still feared for my life. For months, I slept fully clothed on the sofa in my new townhouse. I installed double locks on the doors. I had left in such a hurry that I took nothing with me except the clothes and necessary items I could cram into my compact station wagon. I even forgot our dog.

Standing in the empty living room of the townhouse, I felt a hole where my heart should be. Gone. Everything was gone—my husband, my clothes, my life, even our dog. I watched my children play on the floor with the few toys I'd brought from home, and I felt like I was standing in the shadow of death. I didn't even have furniture. I knew I wouldn't get my furniture until our house sold, but I managed to find a full-sized mattress. The kids and I slept on it every night for weeks. We sat on the floor and ate on cardboard boxes we'd hurriedly tossed my dishes in when we left. Several weeks later, my furniture arrived.

Sadness and grief became constant companions. I grieved the loss of my husband, the loss of our marriage, the loss of security, and the loss of my dog and my friends. I had moved to a new city not knowing anyone except my father, who was too busy with his own life and family to help us.

In the beginning, I cried out of loneliness and self-pity. There was not a soul who seemed to care. I couldn't bring myself to go the short distance to a nearby church for help. I found it harder and harder to function.

Finally, I found work as a part-time secretary and began bringing home a small paycheck, but it wasn't enough. With David in school and Donnie in daycare, I could barely pay for the day-to-day expenses—daycare, rent, food, and the car payment.

I was too afraid to fight for child support, so I chose to get food stamps. Depression broke through as summer turned into fall. Soon the Christmas season was upon us, and try as I might, I couldn't save enough to buy my children Christmas presents and decorations. I wasn't concerned about myself—I just wanted to be sure I could give my children a couple of toys.

About a week before Christmas, an acquaintance saw our plight and bought us a nice-sized Christmas tree. The boys and I decorated it with ornaments from our past. I tried not to let them see the pain in my eyes as I hung each ornament with care.

Christmas drew closer, and I noticed the needles on the tree began to dry out. I hoped the tree would at least make it to Christmas Day, but two days before, it turned completely brown, and the needles dropped like snow.

"Mama, the tree's dying," said David, my seven-year-old. I watched sadness grow in my child's eyes as he helped me take down the decorations. Together we silently lugged the dead tree to the curbside. Sparkling lights, brightly colored wreaths, and beautifully decorated Christmas trees were in every apartment, and we were forced to take down the last remnant of our celebration of Christ's birth.

That Christmas morning we sat cross-legged on the gold shag carpet while the boys opened their small packages. One toy—a bubble gum machine—failed to work. I fought back tears as David tried to fix it for his brother. Like our lives, the bubble gum machine just couldn't be fixed. Trying not to cry, I wrapped my arms around my children. As I stood in the middle of the apartment, David said, "It's all right, Mama, we'll make it."

Tears slid down my cheeks, and I whispered, "Help us, Lord."

Later, a co-worker who had noticed how low I'd sunk, brought a small orange-colored ball of fur to our home. I fell in love with the tabby immediately, and he quickly won a place in the kids' hearts. Almost immediately, I placed him in Donnie's lap.

My little boy's eyes widened and a smile curved upwards as he put his head on the kitten's stomach.

"What are you doing, honey?" I asked, watching Donnie's strange reaction to the newcomer. His eyebrows furrowed in deep thought, and then he said, "My kitty has swallowed a motorcycle! I hear it in his tummy!"

I did something that day that I hadn't done in months. I laughed out loud. The sound of my children's laughter exploded like a rose in bloom, and the fragrance of joy renewed my faith. I knew, within my heart, that God had answered my prayers, and my little family would make it.

Looking back, I realized the Lord warned me in the dream not to scream, but to be calm and tell my husband I loved him. I truly believe that the reason I am still here is because I obeyed God. As a result, I have been able to see all my children grow into young adults. I am grateful I trusted His still, small voice.

The Voice

By L. Pat Williams
Chicago, Illinois, United States

B oy, did I ever have a "nudge" from God!
   It happened in late July 1999. I was packing to leave town (Chicago) for a family trip to New York (Long Island). As normal, I thought nothing more of the process, other than just trying to complete the task, and I practically "wrecked" my bedroom to do so.

Anyway, as I was tossing shorts, deodorant, toothpaste, hair products, underwear, and everything else I deemed "important" into my traveling case, I heard a small voice in my head, out of the blue, say: "Lie down."

I don't remember being exceptionally tired, as it was early evening, and I was determined to finish the exhaustive task, but I did as I heard in my head: I lay down in my bed.

I remember lying on my back, at first thinking, *Why am I lying down? I must be crazy! I need to finish packing and clean up this mess.*

But, as I lay there—alone, I felt a "presence" enter my bedroom, which, of course, inspired me to get up and get up fast. But by then it was too late.

The visiting "aura" in the room was paralyzing. I could do nothing but dart my eyes around the room, but mostly, I gazed at the ceiling. The sheer power emanating from this unseen feeling was awesome, and I must admit, a little unnerving.

Anyway, as I continue to lay belly-up, I heard that same small voice in my head again. But this time it was overpowering, deliberate, and undeniably not my voice.

No, the voice did not resonate like those of God-imitation voices prefabricated by Hollywood movies or commercials. It wasn't that "big booming" or frightening "flesh-fall-off-the-bone" monologue. It was tranquil, still, amazingly calm, but yet very terse. The voice, now the most dominate thing in my head, proclaimed, "When you get back from New York, your life will never be the same again."

Ultra-brazen and foolishly gutsy, I dared ask, of course non-verbally, *What does this mean?*

The voice responded quite matter-of-factly, "When you get back, turn in your resignation."

Now, not only am I not even thinking about work on the advent of my family vacation, but I am certainly not entertaining any thoughts of quitting my job.

What?

I had just received a promotion to supervisor over one of Chicago's more prominent and lucrative publishing companies' cashier department. There was a promised raise on the way. Not to mention the fact I was still 20-something and living at home with a middle-aged dad whose own "prosperous" salesman job abruptly ended after almost 23 years of service, leaving his head on the corporate-downsizing guillotine—which basically meant that quitting my job would leave only Mother's income, albeit a nice income, but still, leave only Mother's income to maintain a household of three.

Please! And you think I'm really going to quit my job? Turn in a resignation letter? OK. Right.

But the voice—the nudge—wouldn't leave me alone. "It is your time. It is time for your destiny."

After several moments thinking I needed to get my head checked once this "thing" was over and mentally resisting the voice, I somehow found solace in the statement, "It is your time. It is time for your destiny."

It dawned on me that I had recently completed my first-ever book after months of research, nights of sipping coffee, days at work feeling tired because of it, weekends, and friends blown-off because of my pet project.

Maybe indeed it was my time! Maybe it was my time to really take my "hobby" seriously. *But to leave my now-more-than-ever needed job...You can't be serious.*

But the voice was serious. And so serious, it reiterated its original command, "When you get back, turn in your resignation." At that moment, the "presence" seemed to evaporate. I was free. I was, as they say, a "loosed woman." I sat straight up in my bed. And wondered what had really just befallen me.

Days later, I was basking in the Long-Island sun, dining off shore of the Amityville boarding docks, and feeling as eerie as the horrific tale of the New York village itself—not because of Amityville, but Chicago.

Chicago loomed with uncertainties as I shuddered to think of the "visitation" I had a few days earlier. But, as time and fate would have it, Chicago was now the advent.

As I left New York and then stepped foot on Chicago soil, I waited incessantly, nervously for that voice to return. But it didn't. Not this day anyway. Not even on the morrow. I was safe.

Twirling in the office chair of my coveted and cherished position, hungry and set to attack the lunch on my desk, I chomped down. Chewing and turning the pages of my company's product, I delighted myself as much in the product's daily news as in that day's daily bread that sat before me.

Normal.

Just one more chomp and flip of the page before I am back on the clock.

Chomp.

Flip.

Voice.

Paralyzed.

Hunched motionless over my desk. The presence—the voice—speaks. A supernatural tap on the shoulder. A surrealistic memento, crippling with each moment. "Turn in your resignation. It is your time."

But this time, there's more instruction.

"Make September 1 your last day."

Again, alone. But this time I am silently praying to God that it isn't Him that I hear or that at least someone would call my extension or knock on my office door.

But that doesn't happen. The presence and its sidekick voice leaves.

I'm a wreck! I rush over to my computer and begin typing up "the resignation."

I'm angry, hoping the thrown-together memo addressed to the attention of the company's upper management will alone satisfy the voice. One more keystroke. It is finished.

OK? I've written the resignation! Now, can I go on with my life?

No voice. Days pass and miraculously, no voice.

Heaven is pleased. I am pleased.

I have conquered! I wrote the resignation, which remained fossilized on the computer's hard drive. Apparently, this calmed the voice, as well as my nerves, since the resignation never left my office. I was safe.

At least another day.

Going about normal day-to-day activities at the office, I am paralyzed. Standing, but paralyzed. Surprisingly getting used to these events, the voice speaks.

"Turn in your resignation."

But today is a different day. I am not going out like a punk this time. Alone, I speak out. I am the voice.

"No way! With all that's going on in my life—no way!
But God if this is really You demanding such a thing from me,
then You're gonna have to prove it! Only then will I turn in the
resignation." *Right on!*

The voice likes the challenge.

"I will give you three signs from three different entities."

Cool. But entities? OK...I guess.

The presence and the voice leave. The phone rings. Not
being superstitious, I don't take incoming phone calls as signs
from the Lord. So I answer. It's my friend, Janine. Normal.

"Hey, girl!" She says. She invites me to a prayer conference that just hit town. It is hosted by Atlanta's eloquent and
charismatic Bible teacher, Pastor Creflo Dollar.

I like him, so I go.

He teaches, preaches, and works Holy Ghost-inspired
miracles. No signs. Then...he stops.

He says, "There's someone here tonight, and God told
you to do something...You better do it!"

He continues teaching, preaching, and working miracles.

Of course, I tell myself, *God has told everybody at some
point to "do something." Love your neighbor. Love your wife.
Love your husband. Love your brother. Love your sister. Love
your enemy. Love yourself. Love Him.*

OK, voice, nice try...but I ain't falling for it!

I go home. I go to bed. I wake up earlier than usual. I sit
on my bed. I turn the TV on.

A little brunette, Southern-drawl speaking, lady minister, Joyce Meyers, is teaching from the same Bible passage as
the Man of God last night.

A little creepy. But I'm still sleepy. *Big deal.*

Then she stops her televised message with a deafening
break of silence.

She says, "There's somebody out there watching this program right now, and God has told you to 'do something.' You had better go do it!"

OK, now I'm scared!

I turn the TV off and head for the shower and another day's labor at my predestined crossroad.

Once at the office, I get a call from my best friend—an accountant (now my personal accountant)—who works on the executive floor. She invites me to "go to church" with her that evening. I have no objections.

So we go to church and her pastor, (now my pastor) who remembered my name due to the few times I had visited her church, calls me up before the entire congregation.

"Sister Lucy, I have a word from the Lord for you!"

My heart would have collapsed if it wasn't beating to a pulse strong enough to pound a hole in my chest. My mind is racing, and my knees are quaking. I walk up to the center aisle of the church. All eyes are on me.

The pastor, exhibiting a sincere warmth in his eyes says, "Lucy, God has instructed you to do a specific thing. He is testing your obedience."

I can't take it all in as my mind registers three different people in three different settings saying the same thing! The *same* thing the voice said.

I collapse as the pastor's strong instructions mingled with impromptu prayer fades into echoes. Then I'm back and being consoled by my friend and members of the church. I know now what I have to do. I am resolved. Come hell or high water, I have to turn in the resignation. I have to quit my job. I have to get my head checked. Regardless, I have to quit my job.

My hands tremble as I turned the key in the lock of my office door. I enter and sit at the computer, pondering my fate. I boot it and eventually log on. It seems to have taken an eternity just to do that! *Can I really go through with this?*

The voice.

"Yes."

So, I do. I turn in my resignation much to the chagrin and apprehension of my family and friends. But, I do it! I am no longer a title, an employee, and in so many ways, myself. The voice was right. My life will never be the same again.

****

September 1, 1999, came and went—and days of frustration, anger, bitterness, and "unnecessary" lack also went by. Soon enough, I was broke, out of work, and scraping up temp jobs and pennies just to keep from drowning in the storm. I reunited with my lost love—writing.

I started to lose count of minutes, hours, and eventually days. These were my days with God. I felt like Moses must have felt—like I had somehow wandered onto a mountain, heard the voice of God, only desiring to see Him as a way of knowing that He was real and truly with me. But, just as with Moses, He only gave me a "glimpse" of Himself and left me with no greater task other than to write everything down.

So I did. But even Moses eventually had to come down from the mountain and dig what was taking place in the camp. Must I say it?

So did I.

A phone call made me flee from the mountaintop. "Hello."

It's my best friend who still works at the old place. With urgency she says, "Guess what?"

I respond, but am not really sure why. "No, what?"

"Your boss, (she says his name, but for wisdom's sake here, I omit it), was let go!"

"What?"

"Yeah—they let him go. He had been stealing company money. And, every time we'd get into meetings, he would try to bring up your name. But it didn't work. You've been gone since September. And since September, money has been missing and none of his stuff has balanced out."

Since September? I thought to myself as I looked at the calendar hanging over the kitchen banister. *It's late October.* At this point, I zoned out, trying to figure out where I, the time, or both I and the time had gone over the past month.

Then I hear my friend say, "You know what? That was really God who told you to leave this job."

Jolted back to reality. "What?"

She carries on. "Yeah, when you told everybody back in August that you were leaving because God told you, I was like, 'OK…but just be sure you're hearing from God.'"

"But, I tell you, (your boss) was setting you up all the time. When the auditors were here, it was like none of the money in your department was balancing. But because you had records of all the stuff you did and money kept coming up missing even after you were gone, they knew it was (your boss)!"

Startled beyond belief, I couldn't find the words. But my friend did and said them for me.

"Girl, if you had stayed a minute past September 1st, you would have been caught up in that mess. Did you know (the new cashier supervisor) was taken down to the police station for questioning? She told me that the police officer pulled her to the side and told her, 'You're lucky you passed your test (lie detector test), because your boss was trying to frame you.'"

Taken aback, I said, "Wait a minute, how could he try to frame her when she's only had the position for a little over a month?"

My friend replied. "Exactly. So imagine if you had stayed. You know he was definitely going to try to put that on you. Especially since that $70,000 came up missing from (the charity event the company sponsored every year) last month."

"Wow." It was the only thing left to say.

So our conversation ended. But my situation did not. Of course, I was grateful to "the voice," because if it had not been for its words of wisdom, my name would have been slandered and marred, but most of all, I would have been fighting for my integrity to keep out of jail from a bogus frame up. I was grateful.

But it wasn't complete. The voice had also said "it was my time." I interpreted that as being the ultimate road to fulfill my childhood dream of being a writer. Since the time my third-grade teacher, Mrs. Berry said, "Lucille, I've never seen a child write like you. You should become a writer when you grow up," I had purposed to grow up and write.

She had been astounded that I used the word "careened" and used it in its right context in my book report. She had asked me if I knew what the word meant. I did. And I told her. She had been amazed.

But all of that meant nothing now. I had a pile of rejection letters for the book I had just finished writing. Those letters seemed to come faster than bills in the mail. I was still broke and broken. So "the voice" and I had some unfinished business.

And it was the voice from there on that led me to the great job of being a soup and sandwich maker/sometimes cashier and stock girl at a downtown deli. Free food! It was a blessing and quite humbling.

The voice then led me to another Chicago news publication. That led me to the editor's office asking her to "give me a shot."

I was a proofreader.

Then the voice led me to freelancing for local entertainment magazines and specialty publications.

I was a stringer.

The voice led me on. I wound up at a senior news-medical journal.

I was a reporter.

The voice continues to lead me.

Roughly three years later, I am now a news contributor at a Chicago FM radio station.

"The voice" led me to the ultimate destiny.

He led me to my voice.

He gave me a voice.

Saving An Angel

By Jozette Aaron
Oshawa, Ontario, Canada

Winter storms are one sure way of bringing business to the labor and delivery department of the regional hospital in my small community.

I am an obstetrical RN, and I work 12-hour shifts—both nights and days. It was December 20th, and the landscape wore its customary white cloak while a veneer of glare ice coated the roads. The wind blew the snow around causing whiteout conditions. Traffic was at a standstill.

The unit was busy for most of the day. Babies wanting to greet Santa in person terminated their lease and worked their way into the world, screaming in victory as they vacated the womb. The staff was so busy that breaks were not an option. We had gotten to the point that if we didn't laugh, we'd cry with exhaustion and the myriad of emotions that drained our reserve.

Once the last baby had been born and a head count done, we were amazed to find that we had delivered 12 newborns in a nine-hour period—and *still* had three hours to work.

We cleaned and restocked the unit, then sat to have coffee, food, and anything else we needed.

The team leader reassessed the workload and decided to send one nurse home early. We had previously decided that whenever there is an opportunity to leave early, which is a rare occurrence, that we'd go in rotation. Thank goodness it was my turn! I collected my gear and dragged on boots, coat, and scarf.

"You're not going to stand out in that mess and wait for the bus, are you?" one of the nurses asked.

"No...not this morning. I'm callin' a cab. I'm so tired I'd fall asleep in the bus shelter. At least the cab driver will wake me up, especially if he wants to get paid. I'll see ya tonight."

"See ya tonight. Try to get a good sleep. If this storm keeps up, there'll be plenty more where this shift came from," the team leader quipped as I headed down the corridor towards the elevators.

Just as I was about to press for the down elevators, one came up. The doors slid open, and I had my first encounter with Dayne Brown, a mid-20's female, slightly shorter than average in height, with thick, short, curly auburn hair—very pretty and very obviously pregnant—frowning in concentration as she coped with a contraction. She looked into my eyes, and at that precise moment, I knew this was trouble.

I told her who I was and asked if she needed a wheelchair to get to the admissions desk. She assured me she could walk, but I walked with her just in case.

"I thought you were goin' home," one of my co-workers said as she watched me escorting the patient to the admissions desk.

"I will, I will... I just want to get this lady admitted and..."

"Go on. Go home. How often do we get to leave early? We'll look after her."

Mrs. Brown looked at me in a particularly pleading manner, as though asking me not to leave her. I patted her gently on her shoulder and reassured her that she would be well taken care of.

"Are you coming back later?" she asked, a small moan of discomfort escaping her lips.

I felt her abdomen to assess the contraction and again felt that this lady would be a concern.

"I will be back tonight…around 7:00 p.m., OK? I'll come look for you…*and* the baby. If you keep having contractions like these, you'll be delivering this angel in no time."

She thanked me for my kindness, and after reassuring her again, I left…though I could feel her frightened blue-gray eyes following my departure.

Fear is synonymous with labor. I have dealt with laboring women, their coping skills, and their lack of. I couldn't understand why this one woman haunted me as I hailed a taxi to take me home.

The taxi slid to a silent stop in front of me. I was so weary that had the taxi veered just a little, it would have run me over, and I wouldn't have cared. I climbed into the musty interior and sank down onto the cracked leather of the back seat—eyes heavy with the need for sleep, my mind searching for a reason for my anxieties.

The phone was ringing when I entered my apartment, and I dashed to catch it before the answering machine clicked on.

"Hello…?" I said breathlessly. "No. I don't need any more magazines, thank you," I said and promptly hung up, thus avoiding the prolonged sales pitch slowly making its way through the receiver. I started to dial the hospital just to check on Mrs. Brown, but sleep beckoned to me. Shrugging out of my coat and boots, I headed for the bathroom instead.

I took a long hot bath and, after snuggling into comfy flannel pajamas, I went into the kitchen to make a cup of cocoa. As I stood at the stove, whipping the chocolate into a thick, frothy treat, my mind once again began its obsession with Mrs. Brown.

"That's it!" I said into the silence. "I'm gonna call and see what's up. Otherwise I'll never get to sleep. I *hate* when I do this," I spoke into the silence as I reached for the phone.

"Mrs. Brown has gone home on a pass. She'll be back when she is more established in labor," the secretary informed me.

I breathed an audible sigh of relief and, taking my cocoa with me, went into my bedroom where I turned on the TV to watch the news while I sipped the steaming brew.

When sleep finally claimed me, I was already halfway there, and I slept soundly until the clock radio wooed me awake with music some nine hours later.

I ate a light dinner of a salad and sandwich before leaving for work. I had gotten into the habit of doing this, because you never knew when you would be able to have anything to eat, let alone get a break, once your shift began.

I made my snack and collected the usual junk food and placed it all in my satchel. I then went to get dressed and decided to give my wallet a break by taking the bus back to work. The snow was still falling in an eerily silent sort of way, and I felt like the only person on the planet as I walked carefully to the bus shelter. I didn't have to wait long before seeing the empty conveyance slowly making its way to pick me up.

"Goin' to work?" the familiar driver asked.

"Yep," I responded, as I took a seat directly across from him so we could catch up on each other's news. He had been driving this route for as long as I've been traveling on it, so we often chatted when there weren't too many passengers on board.

Before too long, he halted the bus mid-street to allow me a shorter walk to the main entrance of the hospital. Thanking him, I waved good-bye and made my way up the sidewalk. As I entered the nurse's lounge, the staff going off duty informed me that all was still reasonably quiet. There were only two women admitted, and they were in labor.

"Should be a better night than last night. Have a good one," they said as I left them to go to the team center for report.

Approaching the desk, I read the names of the women in labor and the progress they were making. I took a seat and listened to the short report. Mrs. Brown was discharged; she did not return from her pass. I was not assigned either patient but made team leader instead. This was customary when you were working your third 12-hour night shift in a row.

The first part of the night crawled by slowly. The laboring women progressed slowly but steadily, and by midnight, they had both delivered. They were taken to the postpartum area a short while later, and the nurses were sent for their breaks.

I was reading the logbook from the previous shift when a voice caught my attention. When I looked up into the eyes of Dayne Brown, the old anxieties returned.

"I think this is *it* this time," she said as a whimper of pain escaped her lips. "I'm glad you're here."

"Let's get you readmitted, and then I'll take you to one of the rooms. Are you OK to sit through the admission process again?" I asked, noticing for the first time that she was quite alone.

She nodded her head in the affirmative and settled clumsily onto the chair, one hand supporting her burgeoning abdomen.

Once she had been readmitted, I bypassed the assessment room and took her directly into a labor room.

"Are you sure she's ready for that room? Why not use the assessment room? She may go home again," came the questions from a few staff returning from their breaks.

"She's going in a room. I have a feeling she'll be staying this time," I informed them as I escorted Dayne to her room, gave her a brief orientation, and helped her change into a hospital gown.

"Can I do anything to help?" a voice inquired from the doorway.

"Yes. Take over team leading. I'm going to take care of Mrs. Brown."

"Are you sure? This is your third—"

"Positive. Just change the schedule to show the change. Call Dr. Norman and let him know his patient is here," I answered.

After settling Dayne into bed and placing her on the fetal monitor, I went out to the desk to ask the secretary to place the routine orders for laboring mothers with the lab. Shortly afterwards, a lab tech came and drew the necessary vials of blood. I checked the monitor readout and saw a slight elevation in the fetal heart rate, but was not overly concerned, as Dayne had normal values when I did her vital signs.

"She's probably a little dehydrated," I thought to myself as I went in search of juice and water for her.

When I returned, Dr. Norman was standing near her bed, talking with her about her options for pain relief.

"Have you examined her yet?' he asked me as I set a tray of various refreshments on the counter.

"Not yet. I thought you'd prefer to do it so you'd know where she's at right now. I'll get a glove for you."

After the exam, Dr. Norman informed me of her progress and left further orders. "Her membranes haven't ruptured as yet, and the baby's head is pretty high so…watch her for now. See if her labor picks up. Call me in a couple of hours. I'll be on my pager."

Dayne's labor improved. Her contractions were more intense, a consistent pattern had formed, and she was asking for something for pain. I gave her an injection of Demerol, the medication of choice for early labor. Shortly afterwards, she dozed off. I read the monitor strip and, although the fetal heart rate was still slightly elevated, it was in the high normal range.

"She's sleeping right now, so I'm goin' for coffee. Can I get anyone else coffee or something?" I asked as the team leader inquired about Mrs. Brown.

"Go ahead. Take a break while you can."

"I'll be back in 15 minutes then," I said as I left the unit.

When I got back to Dayne, she was very uncomfortable, sweating, and a bit pale. She was breathing too quickly, and I coached her into a better breathing pattern to keep her from hyperventilating.

"I want an epidural—please help me—" she begged.

I'm going to start your IV and then we'll get your epidural, OK?"

She said nothing, allowing me access to her arm which she held rigid with pain. She looked at me with that anxiety-provoking stare, and I returned a reassuring glance but felt that I needed to act quickly.

The anesthetist came up shortly after being paged and inserted her epidural. Twenty minutes later, Mrs. Brown was asleep, and her baby's heart rate was in a better range of normal. Dr. Norman checked in and, satisfied that all was well, left for home to be called when she was ready to deliver.

When Dayne woke up an hour or so later, I examined her cervix, and she had progressed to five centimeters dilatation. She was very happy that this would be over soon—on her way to the 10 centimeters needed to deliver. I felt differently. The fetal heart rate was tachycardic—beating faster than what was normal. I took Dayne's temperature, and it was elevated, as well. I increased the drip rate on her IV to rapidly infuse a large amount of fluid and paged Dr. Norman.

"I'm on my way in."

I felt my anxiety level skyrocket as I hung up the phone— that familiar gut crunch that never let me down now all but doubling me over in pain. Dayne was in trouble. I collected the necessary items needed to prepare her for a cesarean section delivery and then went to talk with her.

"I'm going to put a Foley catheter in—just to keep your bladder empty," I explained as I went about positioning her for the procedure. I examined her afterwards and was disappointed that she was the same five centimeters. Her cervix hadn't changed.

Dr. Norman arrived just as I completed the exam and, when informed that she had made no progress, ordered a Pitocin drip to increase the level of the labor-inducing hormone in her body and give her better contractions.

"I think she needs a section," I whispered as we left the room together.

"It's too soon to make that call. See what the 'pit' does for her contractions."

"The baby isn't coping too well. The heart rate is already at 175 beats per minute. I increased her fluids, but it didn't help much."

"Keep the IV running at 150 ml an hour. Let's just wait for now," he concluded and walked away, effectively cutting off any further suggestions over what *he* should do!

I sat at the bedside watching Dayne sleep. Her skin was pink with fever, her eyelids moving. Every now and then a whimper would escape through lips now parched and dry. I placed my hand on her swollen abdomen, silently soothing the angel within.

"Hang in there, Little One," I said softly as I gently palpated for any signs of a worthy contraction. I glanced at the monitor. The heart rate continued to climb.

Dr. Norman appeared in the doorway, a worried look on his face.

"You're pretty worried about her aren't you? Why? I mean, I know there's fetal tachycardia, but you see that with an elevated maternal temp. What is causing you so much concern? The 'pit' is bringing her contractions back."

"I just have a gut feeling that this baby is in trouble. Yes, the monitor shows the elevated heart rate, but it's also starting to show a decrease in the variability pattern. The line is a bit flat. She needs a section!"

"OK. Let's give her another half hour and—"

"Now, Dr. Norman!" I said with conviction. "You already know that another half hour won't change anything. She's a pretty sick lady, and I am afraid for her baby."

"Make the call. I'll go change."

The call was to the Operating Room—a "stat" c-section was to be done. I called the necessary staff in to help transport the patient. The jostling of the bed and equipment awakened Dayne. I explained the necessity of delivering her baby and got a consent form signed.

"Is my doctor here?" she asked in a fever-parched voice.

"He's going to meet us in the OR and will explain everything to you there—answer your questions—and get you comfortable. Is there anyone you'd like me to call?" I asked, noticing once again that she was still quite alone. I didn't remember seeing any visitors since she arrived.

"No, there's no one," was all she said.

Down in the OR, I set up the infant resuscitation table, called the nursery to alert them of the baby's imminent arrival, and paged the pediatrician stat to the OR. Dayne's epidural was topped-off to afford a high enough block for the incision. Her abdomen was scrubbed with a disinfectant, dried, and draped with sterile sheeting. The pediatrician arrived just as the incision into the abdomen was made.

When Dr. Norman sliced into the uterus and then the amniotic sac, a purulent stench filled the air. He lifted a limp, lifeless newborn from its murky environment, cut the cord, and handed her to me. I quickly carried her to the resuscitation table, her body hot and slippery wet with green amniotic fluid. The pediatrician and I worked to elicit her first weak, bubbly cry.

"Take her to the NICU, and I'll meet you there—bag her while enroute."

I hooked a small black resuscitation bag, used to administer puffs of oxygen through a mask when squeezed, to the cylinders of oxygen located on the transport incubator. I gave Dayne a quick peek at her daughter and told her she'd be in the nursery. Dayne would have to go to the ICU for 48 hours post-op so she could be watched closely.

"That was a pretty bad case of chorioamnioitis," Dr. Norman said as I made to leave the OR with my precious bundle. "How did you know she was so full of infection?"

"I just had a gut feeling about her—the first time I met her. Even though her symptoms were leaning more towards dehydration and her water hadn't broken before now—anyway, I gotta get this angel to the NICU."

I thanked everyone for assisting and headed out the door. Dr. Norman stopped me one last time.

"Good call!" he said.

"The gut never lies!"

Morning of the Snake

By Darlene Zagata
Uniontown, Pennsylvania, United States

When I was about nine years old, I remember my aunt having a hunch that may have saved my uncle's life. We lived in West Virginia at the time in a little out-of-the-way town. My cousins and I were getting ready for school, while my aunt was in the kitchen making breakfast.

My aunt called us downstairs to eat as she filled the table with hot, steaming pancakes, eggs, and crisp bacon. Our mouths were already watering as the wonderful aroma filled the house.

We ran to the table and began gobbling down our food as my aunt admonished us for eating too fast. Our mothers came to the table with their coffee and remarked what a lovely day it was and that they should do some gardening.

After finishing breakfast and taking our dishes to the sink, we gathered our belongings and headed for the door, followed by my Aunt Lora who always waited outside until we were all safely on the school bus.

But this morning, as the screen door was opened, my youngest cousin jumped back and screamed. Lying on the porch right in front of the doorstep was a copperhead snake. Our mothers hurried us all back inside the house while my aunt searched for something to use to kill the snake.

Aunt Lora grabbed the ax my uncle always used for chopping wood and headed out the door to kill the snake. After quickly disposing of the creature, she ushered us all off to the bus warning us all to be very careful, just saying that she had an odd feeling about the day.

Later when I returned from school, I would learn more about what happened next.

My uncle had gone to the little store down the road to get some flour, since my aunt and my mother planned on doing some baking later that day. When he returned, he sat down to eat his breakfast before getting ready for work.

Normally he rode in a carpool with a few other men from the factory, and it was his friend, Ed's, turn to drive that day.

Aunt Lora told her husband about the snake that had been on the porch and how she had an odd feeling that something about the day was going to go dreadfully wrong. My Uncle David told her that she was just being silly and that it was not odd to see snakes in the area at that time of year.

But she insisted it wasn't just the appearance of the snake that was bothering her, but that she was overcome with a fear of impending doom. She asked him to just humor her and not go to work that day.

"I can't just take the day off work because you have a feeling," he said.

Still, my aunt continued to press him to stay home.

"Well, if you insist on going to work, then at least drive your own car. It would make me feel a little better," she said.

Uncle David finally gave in and agreed to take his own car. "OK, I'll have to call Ed and tell him that I have something to do after work. I don't want to get him all riled up with this feeling of yours."

My uncle made the phone call to his friend, making an excuse to take his own car. He asked Ed if he would like to ride with him instead today, but Ed said that he would just pick up the other guys as usual and that he would ride with my uncle next week when it was his turn for the carpool.

With that settled, Uncle David went upstairs to get dressed for work. But even as he was on his way out the door, Aunt Lora was still instructing him to be very careful.

The day continued uneventfully, and my mother and aunt did some gardening and baking as they had planned. They enjoyed the benefits of the beautiful weather as they tended to the garden and filled the house with the scent of freshly baked bread and cookies.

Soon we were home from school and the day was progressing normally. My aunt began to think that perhaps she was just being silly and that her fears had been unfounded after all.

Uncle David usually arrived home from work about two hours after we returned from school, and since no one had heard anything unusual, there was no reason to worry. We were allowed some fresh-baked cookies and then sat down to do our homework. Afterward, we went outside to play.

Soon my uncle was home from work, safe and sound, and Aunt Lora began to relax. Before long, my mother called us to come in and get cleaned up since supper would soon be done.

Then, just as we sat down at the table to eat our meal, the phone rang. It was Ed's wife calling from the hospital. There had been an accident—a pileup on the road with several cars involved. Ed had a concussion, some broken ribs, and some cuts and bruises, but he would be all right. The two other men in the car sustained minor injuries also—one man had a broken leg and the other a broken wrist and dislocated shoulder. Although they were all injured, thank God no was killed or critically injured.

My aunt later said she felt her heart drop to her feet at that moment. Her feeling had been right all along. She had known that something was going to happen that day.

As my uncle hung up the phone, he looked at his wife and said, "How did you know?"

"I didn't. I just had a terrible feeling that something was wrong," she answered.

"Your feeling may have very well saved my life," he said as he hugged his wife.

We were all very relieved that my uncle was not in the accident and that the men who were would be OK. My aunt and uncle went to the hospital later that evening to visit my uncle's co-workers and to relate the story of his wife's hunch. Aunt Lora felt that God had warned her in some inexplicable way, and Uncle David decided he would take his wife's "feelings" a little more seriously in the future.

Deer Helen, This is God

By Helen Kay Polaski
Milan, Michigan, USA

I guess I've always had nudges from God—not about every-thing, mind you, but about enough things that you'd think I'd be paying closer attention by now. Sometimes I'm on my toes; other times when God shoots a warning my way, I can't see it for what it is, or I react like a total idiot. Go figure.

Three times in the past seven years God has seriously nudged me, and I have only Him to thank that I listened. I'm sure there have been plenty of other times when I wasn't so inclined, but since I'm still here, I can only assume the other times weren't life and death situations.

The first time, it was very weird. It was mid-spring and close to midnight. I'd taken advantage of a nearby grocery store's new 24-hour open policy and gone shopping after my three children had gone to bed. My husband had been working long hours and didn't get home until after 8:00 p.m., so I figured it would be the perfect time to take my coupons, and without little ones, I could take my time. As soon as he walked in, I walked out.

Three and a half hours later, my car loaded down with two weeks worth of groceries, I started the 12-mile return trip. It was late, and as I tend to be nervous about driving alone on the expressway that late at night, I took the service drive. I was more comfortable with the idea of waking a poor unsuspecting homeowner and taking the chance I might know them than accepting help from a complete stranger on the highway should I run into trouble.

A thick, gray fog had rolled in while I was shopping, and driving conditions were not the best. Expressway traffic usually doesn't slow down no matter what the weather, and I was determined to putz the rest of the way home.

At first, visibility was nil. But since there was no one else on the road, I took my time. My main concern wasn't arriving home later than planned, but rather arriving all in one piece.

As I drove through a deserted intersection, I detected a break in the fog. Sure enough, within minutes the fog had lifted to a point where only minute wisps snaked across the road before me. The break lasted for nearly a half mile. I relaxed a bit and, quite naturally, my foot lowered on the accelerator.

It was late, and I really could think of nothing but lying down on my bed and resting my weary body. It had been a long day with the children, and running around the grocery store had really taken a toll.

Suddenly, out of nowhere, a thought shot through my head: *Slow down—Now!* The feeling I had was identical to that of being a little child and hearing your mother's voice warn you away from a speeding car or a growling dog. I immediately knew I was in danger and did what I was told. I didn't even consider not slowing down—the voice was that adamant.

I started to brake, and grocery bags tipped off the back seat. Before I had come to a rolling stop, the fog descended again, and seeing anything beyond my windshield was impossible.

Trembling, I pushed my brake foot to the floor mat and came to a complete stop. For some reason, I rolled down my window. A faint tapping noise echoed eerily in the fog, and a snuffling, like a large dog might make, resounded close to my ear. Of course, now I was thinking some maniac dog was going to attack me in the middle of nowhere, and I quickly rolled up my window.

I must have sat there for several minutes before the fog lifted enough for me to see the faint glow of red taillights not 10 feet in front of me. I shook my head and whispered, "Thank You, God."

But as the fog continued to rise, my smile faded, and my heartbeat quickened. Had my window still been open, I could have touched the creatures that had been making the snuffling noises. At least a dozen whitetail deer milled around on the road between and around our cars—apparently confused by the fog. Had I not slowed down when I did, I'm sure I would be dead today.

The second warning came in the middle of the day and totally out of the blue. At the time, I was a reporter for *The Milan News.* Every Tuesday morning I was expected to arrive at the printer no later than 9:00 a.m. sharp. That was a tough order because, invariably, Tuesday morning was the day everything went wrong. This day, just as on the previous Tuesday, nothing went right. I was running late. To make up for my tardiness, I had the pedal to the floor. It was about 10:20 a.m., and I should have been at the office nearly an hour and a half before. I came to a complete stop at the railroad crossing, then gunned my car in the half mile straightaway about three miles from my destination. I had reached a pretty good clip when a thought zipped through my head like a flash of light: *A deer could jump out, and you'd be dead.*

Why I would think that when it was a bright, sunny day and I was surrounded by cornfields was beyond me, but my heart began to beat so hard that I had no choice but to slow down. I was still traveling a tad above the speed limit when a magnificent buck jumped out from the right of my vehicle and continued across the blacktop, disappearing into the cornfield on my left. I think my left headlight parted the fur on his rump—that's how close I had come to a head-on collision!

Why did I think of a deer jumping out? The only acceptable reason must be that God had sent me a nudge. With one hand over my erratically beating heart, I said, "Thank You, God."

Now by this time, you'd think I was smarter than the average bear. But, believe it or not, the third time really proved to me how stupid a human being can be. I was on the same road, again on a Tuesday. I was rushing. I was behind—so far behind that when I roared around that curve and the thought that a deer would jump out in front of me flashed in my head, instead of slowing down, I looked to the side knowing the deer was there and— What? Here God was giving me a warning, and I thought I was Mario Andretti? Did I think I could outrun it? I don't know. It sounds foolish even now to repeat what I did.

But, for some reason, I felt God was with me and, really, what were the chances God was gonna let me hit a deer this time? After all, He'd spared me twice already.

There was an open field on my right with a smattering of trees along the road—and there was no doubt in my mind that there was a deer in there somewhere and that it really was going to jump out from that side—so far they'd all come from the right. I didn't see anything. I smiled. I actually smiled!

Just then a glimpse of white appeared in the dark trees. Whitetail deer lift their tail when danger is near and when they run. This deer was already in a mile-eating race with the wind as he leaped into the open.

Fear balled in my stomach, and I slammed on my brakes. I skidded onto the gravel on the side of the road and nearly fishtailed but miraculously was able to keep control of the vehicle.

The deer bounded out of the strip of trees and, without looking either way, cut right across the road in front of me. This deer actually leapt over the hood of my vehicle! I saw the underside of his white belly, and all I could think of was those powerful hooves slashing me to ribbons when he landed on my windshield.

I was instantly grateful and relieved when, in fact, the deer's front hooves touched the pavement and in one additional stride it had tucked its back legs in and sailed forward again. As it disappeared into the shadows on the other side of the road, I actually wept—not because I had escaped the deer's hooves and what might have been my own death, but because I had been given a sign, and I hadn't paid close enough attention.

Like a patient and loving father, God was trying to get me safely to my destination, and I, like a spoiled child, thought I knew better.

Have I learned my lesson?

I think so...I hope so. But as a child of God, I know we all do things that don't make sense sometimes. We question when we should accept. We doubt when we should believe.

Since I don't believe in coincidences, I think I was supposed to believe I was infallible for that one instant—perhaps to strengthen my ties with God, perhaps to show me how necessary it is to believe.

This much is certain: from now on, if I even remotely think there's a deer nearby, I'm putting on my brakes!

Daddy, Please Wait For Me

By Del Sylver Bates
Vero Beach, Florida, United States

"Just one more spoonful. Come on, just one more spoonful of applesauce. Then you can rest for the night." Continually these words replay in my mind. They were words spoken through a painted smile on my face while trying to feed my dad one of his last meals before he went home to be with the Lord.

The phone call came on a Thursday afternoon from my friend up north: "I just picked your mom up from the hospital where they admitted your dad."

"For what this time?" I questioned.

"I guess they found out he is bleeding internally," she explained.

"He's been sick for some time, with his heart and other symptoms, but never this—never internal bleeding," I replied. My gut feeling said this time it was serious.

With my family living in another state, it had been very difficult not to be able to run up for every hospital stay. Now my mind began to race. What was I to do? This decision must be guided from above. God, and only God, knew the definite time my dad would stand in His presence, so He would be the only one to tell me if I should go.

Each day the phone calls intensified. With five brothers and sisters and my three grown children living up north, I continually received updates on my dad's condition.

My son spoke words from his heart to help guide mine: "All I can say is, if it were you or Dad, and I lived out of state, I'd be here now."

His words painted a picture of the hospital room precisely in my mind. Through daily prayer, the Lord guided me step by step with His peace.

The first step was my gift shop. Being the owner and only employee of my little shop in our hotel, He showed me I must get things in order. With Easter just around the corner, the Lord directed me to do all that was required in the event I did not return for the busy weekend and employees from the front desk would be called on to lend a hand. "Pay any due bills," He directed. "Leave no strings unattached. Get it all in shape."

"Purchase the ticket," He directed me one morning in my prayer time. Though this was not the day to go, I purchased the ticket for two weeks in advance knowing it could be changed with a quick call.

Daily I began to lay aside outfits for the colder temperatures that awaited me in Michigan. With each phone call from my family and children, my heartstrings pulled tighter and tighter. The most difficult time was when my son put the phone to my dad's ear so I could say hello.

"Del, I'm sick," he said. "This time something is wrong with me."

"You'll be home in no time. You pulled through before— you'll do it again," I responded.

But as I hung up the phone, I knew in my spirit that this time was different. I realized it was not like my dad to admit it was serious.

He would always say, "Don't worry, I'll be OK." Did he have a clue that eternity was just a stone's throw away? Another tug.

Close friends, who had now become like a second family to me in Florida, questioned, "Del what are you going to do this time? Are you going up there?"

My only response was, "When it's time to go, I'll know." Actually, it happened just that way. The next Saturday morning I was awakened with a dream of my worst fear.

In my dream, I arrived up north, and it was too late. I could see my mom sitting in her wheelchair at the end of a long narrow hall. Running as fast as my feet would carry me, I headed on down. Two . . .three . . . four doors away, I could hear wailing from within my dad's room. My mom greeted me and held out her hand. With her body as still as the sea, quietly she spoke, "Daddy has passed on. He's finally at peace. Del, it's OK—it's OK."

That warning during the night was much the same as the mother who knows just when her labor is about to begin. When my husband awoke at 9:00 a.m., my suitcases stood lined up at the door, ready to accompany me on my standby flight.

The plane ride lasted forever. *Daddy, please wait for me*, I pleaded with each beat of my heart.

Inside, the Lord gave me His peace, while explaining that this was all part of the process of life. Gently He led me to the book of Ecclesiastes, showing me in detail that there is a time to be born and, yes, there is a time to die. "I know, Lord," I whispered, "But if You can see it in Your plan, please let me say a final good-bye."

God not only heard my prayers, but He also allowed me a week long journey with my family to feed and comfort my dad in every way. Sadly, the days flew by like falling snow, and my return flight was right around the corner. *What shall I do?* I wondered.

Within that week, my dad had been moved from the hospital to the nursing home and back to the hospital. How could I just pick up and leave the dad who had always put the food on the table…the dad who had said that Santa had forgotten him for Christmas but remembered all six kids…how could I leave?

Knowing that the kiss he blew me each night to say goodnight just might be the last one? How? How could I leave?

Tarrying with the decision before me, I was on my way to see my daughter, Jennifer, early one morning. As I turned on the car radio, I knew the message was just for me. "Honor your father and mother. Honor them not only while you live in their house, but in their ripe old age when they can no longer care for themselves." The pastor on the radio quoted one scripture after the other confirming that we were given our parents for life, not just when we are little and we need them. But all the more, we are to be there when they need us.

My dad did need me. Actually, with my mom unable to drive and her desire to be at my dad's bedside day and night, I knew she needed me, too. Was this program a divine appointment?

The smell of freshly brewed coffee was not strong enough to hold back the tears as I entered my daughter's house. My heels had not even crossed the threshold when words and tears gushed forth. "Grandpa's not doing good. I don't know what I should do. But I just heard this sermon," and on and on I went.

With love, her slender arms opened wide for a much-needed hug as she responded, "Mom, you know what you have to do. No one knows how long Grandpa will be here, so just do whatever your heart tells you."

Her words not only comforted me, but also reassured me that if the Lord had guided me to get here, He was just as capable of providing when I should depart.

Decisively, He did more than that. He gave me a spirit of peace each day as I tried to be a shoulder for my mom, who was struggling with her own aging ailments. Daily, I would wheel her chair beside my dad's bed, where she would grab hold of his hand and reminisce about their last 54 years together. Reality was setting in, but it was better when it took a back seat.

Though I was going through my own moments, I tried desperately to understand what she was facing.

Then four weeks had passed, and I knew it was time to return home.

The smell of hospital food still hung in my mind. The continuous hugs of family and friends left imprints of joy mingled with pain inside. All these memories were in the forefront of my mind as I secured my seatbelt once again for takeoff. But the Lord had directed me back to Florida with a peace, and yet a knowing that I would much too soon stand on this very ground for the final good-bye.

Then one day...there they were—the expected, yet unexpected, words: "They have given Daddy 48 hours." My mother's voice was calm and peaceful.

I knew the Lord had prepared her for this moment. At the same time, I began to understand how He, in His infinite power and wisdom, shuts us down during such a time, because the pain of the loss is so unbearable that it is truly the only way we could handle it.

Here I was again, buckling up on a wing and a prayer.

As the plane ascended, my tears descended. Unable to stop the flow, a caring airline steward gently knelt beside me to see if I was OK, "Is there anything I can do?" she asked.

"Tissues, tissues," I mumbled between my sobs. Finally, when I got a grip on myself, I glanced at my watch: 4:15. Once again I pleaded, *Daddy, please, please wait for me.*

Feelings invaded my being. I was not released with the peace like before. It was strange—like something had been lifted out of my chest. *What was I feeling? Was he gone? But—it hadn't been 48 hours yet. Could it be—?*

Greeted by my sons at the airport, I felt their hugs much warmer than usual, yet their demeanor was kind of cold. Were their gestures telling me what I had felt on that 747 was for real? *Had the Lord already taken my dad by the hand to be with Him?*

"Has anything changed?" I asked. "We are still heading for the hospital, right?" The blank look bounced from Michael, my oldest, to my other son, Brian.

"We...didn't...well, don't know how to tell you." And I knew. No more words—just hugs. Just sobs and sobs.

Then suddenly I blurted out, "The dream! The dream. I wasn't there in the dream, and I didn't make it now. I missed him. I missed saying good-bye."

As the bags of luggage continued to circle round and round, Michael and Brian comforted me. As we left the airport, they informed me that everyone was meeting at my brother, Robert's, house. We, too, were on our way.

Alone in the back seat, I kept hearing the words of disbelief over and over when my body began to quiver inside. Then suddenly, I felt as though someone had placed an electric blanket around me. Peace welled over.

"You were there when he needed you. You were there when he recognized who you were. You were there when he could utter the words 'I love you.'" The words flowed from within.

"Yes, Lord I hear You...the broadcast...the radio that morning...thank You, Lord. You revealed for me to remain and I did, and now I will be able to go forward with mingled tears of sorrow that he is gone, but joy for all the wonderful memories You allowed."

Don't Go

By Vinette Smit
Pretoria, Gauteng, South Africa

About 20 years back, when I graduated from high school, I started working at a branch of a large life insurance company in a rather small town. It was the town of Ermelo situated in the province of Transvaal in South Africa.

My dad got transferred a lot, and that meant we didn't stay long in one place. So I immediately made friends with a large number of people, most of whom were in about the same age group as me.

There wasn't a whole lot to do on weekends and holidays, so we were pretty much left to our own devices and imagination to keep us occupied. There was an old rundown drive-in movie theater in town, but that was about all, so most of the time, we just hung out at each other's houses or went for a milkshake at the local Wimpy.

My best friends, though, were Erna and Marina. We did everything together—including getting into mischief. Marina was a bit older than Erna and I, and she was already married for a year or so. Marina usually took the lead in deciding what we would do on weekends, and the rest of us followed. Erna and I are the same age, so we immediately became so close that we only had to sneak a look at each other to know what the other was thinking!

One day Marina invited me to go with her to visit her parents for the weekend in a neighboring town. Usually she and her husband went to visit, but he was out of town for business, and she didn't like to go on her own. They had gotten their brand new car just the week before, and she wanted to show the car to her folks.

I really wanted to go, but something made me hesitate. The fact that we would be taking the new car was tempting, but the feeling that I shouldn't go was stronger by far. Because I couldn't put the feeling into words, I was even beginning to doubt myself. It was like that sick feeling you get in the pit of your stomach just before something really bad happens, but a lot stronger—but still, nothing you could really put your finger on.

Normally, I would have jumped at the chance to get out of town. Marina was a very good driver, she was a responsible person, and I wanted to get out of the house for a few days. I was still living with my parents, and at that stage, you want to start spreading your wings and become independent.

I don't think I would have had a hard time explaining to my dad or mom where I wanted to go—after all, it was to my friend's parents' home. But I never even asked my parents. I told Marina that I had a previous engagement with other friends and I couldn't go. It was a white lie, because I didn't have anything planned for the weekend. But I didn't think that Marina would take me seriously if I told her I didn't want to go just on account of a weird feeling.

The night after I told Marina I couldn't go, I lay in bed thinking, and I couldn't sleep a wink.

I felt so bad that the next morning I talked to my other friend, Erna, and asked her, "Do you think I'm being silly, or am I just being inconsiderate? Please be honest."

She told me: "Listen to 'your little voice,' because it is trying to tell you something," and then she added, "I think it may even be warning you."

I trusted her judgment and agreed with her on all the points she made. After a lengthy discussion, I decided I had made the right decision not to go, but I still felt a little bad about the lie I told and decided to tell Marina about it first thing Monday morning, even if it meant that she would be disappointed in me.

Time went by and the weekend came to an end, and a normal Monday morning began, except that there was no sign of Marina. Business hours commenced, and the boss called us together unexpectedly. One look at his face told us that something had happened. Erna and I immediately knew that it had to do with Marina's absence.

He told us that Marina was in a car accident just a few hours back. I immediately thought he was going to tell us that she was dead! She was alive, but in a critical condition in hospital.

She had planned to come directly to work from her folks' house that morning. She was running a bit late and was overtaking a car, when the direct sunlight from the rising sun right in front of her blinded her for just a second, and she lost control of the car. The car went off the road and rolled a few times before landing in a deep ditch.

The new car was a total write-off. She wasn't wearing her seatbelt and was thrown clear of the rolling car through the passenger window. According to the police, if there had been a passenger in the car, she probably could not have been thrown clear, and the outcome of the accident would have changed dramatically. For the worse or the better? We will never know. I know I would have been wearing my seatbelt, because I never get in a car without putting my seatbelt on—to me it's automatic, like brushing your teeth in the morning.

While the manager was telling us all about the accident, Erna and I just looked at each other, and although we weren't saying a word, both of us knew that the other was thinking about our last discussion and about my "little voice" that was trying to warn me not to go along on that weekend trip.

Every word we spoke about it a short time ago rang in my ears as I struggled to get control of my emotions. While there was this terrible relief that Marina was alive, I couldn't get over the enormous feeling of thankfulness that I wasn't a passenger in that car on that particular day. I even felt guilty about being so happy to be alive when Marina was in hospital in a critical condition, but I had a second chance in life. All these thoughts and much, much more ran though my mind all at once.

Erna's face reflected the same thoughts.

Needless to say, not much work was done that day—the whole office stood still. The boss even gave us a longer lunch hour to check up on Marina.

We visited Marina in the hospital frequently after that, and she recovered fully. The car was replaced by the insurance company within a week.

We talked about the circumstances of that trip for a long time afterward. Marina said she had also thought it best not to pressure me into coming with her that weekend, though normally she would have tried her best to change my mind, because that is just the kind of person she is. Normally she wouldn't have let up until I changed my mind. But she said she had had an indescribable feeling to just leave it at that. She hadn't thought about it until I brought it up in hospital after the accident.

To this day, Erna and I are still the best of friends. Unfortunately, we lost contact with Marina a few years back, but we will never forget that Monday.

I've never experienced such a strong feeling as the one I had about that weekend again. You can call it what you will—a nudge from God or by any other name. But I'm certain that it was intended as a warning—and by listening to it, it saved my life.

Once Upon A Time

By Dorothy Hill
Potts Camp, Mississippi, United States

"Have you got your night-night eyes on?" I asked the little girl I held in my arms.

She closed her eyes tightly and nodded her head in the affirmative. She shifted her grip a little on the sippy cup held in the crook of her arm and twisted her body in an effort to find that perfect position to go to sleep.

"Good," I said. "I'm getting sleepy, too."

My son-in-law accuses me of spoiling my granddaughter at moments such as this, but I don't pay him any attention. After all, what is a grandmother for? And so she and I quietly rocked back and forth, back and forth, back and forth, until she fell asleep and I became lost in my thoughts.

I came very close to missing moments like this, and I would have if I had not listened to God.

Once upon a time, my life was very uncomplicated. Back in the fall of 1985, I had a good job and had just bought a house a few months before. Not having a husband or children, I mistakenly believed I was in charge of my life. I didn't have to answer to anyone—or so I thought. That's when the Lord told me that it was time.

Time? Time for what? Now was the time, He was telling me, to open my home to children who needed one.

Back in the far reaches of my mind, I always knew that if I ever had a family, it would not be the conventional type. I knew what the Lord was asking of me, but at the age of 35, I wanted no part of it. I didn't want to change my life. I liked it just like it was.

And so began a rather one-sided conversation with God over a period of days, as I tried to convince Him that His timing was wrong.

Do you know what I will have to give up? I argued with Him. I liked being able to go see a movie whenever I wanted. I liked eating at fancy restaurants. I liked seeing plays at the Orpheum Theater in Memphis. Now that I had my Masters and my Specialist degrees, I was ready to do some traveling. I had a nice child-free home with antiques and collectibles. Children were not on my list of things I had time for.

I had sought once before to get involved with children who needed someone. I was turned down by the children's home that my church denomination sponsored. The reason: I was single. *Well, my marriage status has not changed, so why the push now, Lord?*

Since it was very easy to say "no" to nameless, faceless children, God decided to rattle my world a little. A student of mine suddenly wasn't there anymore. I had last seen him in the office the day we were getting out for Thanksgiving holidays. When we came back, he was gone. He and his younger brother were in foster care. God, in His way, had thrown down the gauntlet. Needy children were no longer hypothetical. Now there was a face—a warm body—in the equation.

In December of 1985, I applied to become a foster parent with our county Department of Human Services. The following spring, I received my license.

The antiques and the collectibles are pretty much gone now. The neat little house has been traded for a rambling older home in constant need of repair. Fast food, rather than fancy restaurants, have become more my speed. Movies became matinees or second-runs. *Sesame Street Live* and *Disney on Ice* are the only live productions we've seen except for school plays and talent shows. Travel became short day trips close to home. Since we couldn't travel to exotic locations, we managed to find room for a couple of exchange students from places like Ecuador and Thailand.

Through the years, many children have come and gone—except for three little girls. God allowed me to adopt them.

"Mamaw," said the little girl in my arms, putting an end to my reminiscing and bringing me back to the present. "I not sleepy anymore."

"You're not?" I responded.

"I want to play with you, Mamaw."

"What do you want to play?" She got out of my lap, took my hand, and led me into the living room where cars and dolls and a table and chairs just her size awaited.

"I love you, Mamaw."

I am sure thankful that once upon a time the Lord saw fit to not let my life remain uncomplicated.

The Cat Came Back

By Carole McDonnell
Peekskill, New York, United States

When my husband and I moved into our new house, we discovered we had a mouse problem. The house had been shut up for months while the sale was pending, and during that time, the mice made themselves at home.

During the first month we lived there, we killed five or six of them, but there were always more skittering furballs dashing across the floor.

The never-ending stream of mice might be only a mere bother to someone else, but I was struggling with depression and insomnia that my doctor attributed to a hormonal imbalance. And although sleeplessness and depression are both hard for a new mother, it was made worse by the burden of our mice-infested handyman special.

The house had been cheap compared with other houses in our county, a wealthy bedroom community to the north of New York. My husband and I were not rich, so we were happy to buy the "starter house." We believed in our ability to turn it into our dream house.

But my depression, my husband's sudden job loss, and the rundown aspects of the house were taking their toll. The mouse situation was the last straw.

I could not open a closet or sweep a room without encountering mouse reminders. They were everywhere.

As the baby grew older and learned to crawl, I began to find the situation more and more disheartening. Not only did I feel poor and "stuck," but I worried constantly about our son's health.

My mother was a nurse, and she warned us constantly about the germs mice carry. Her words were meant to be helpful, but visions of bubonic plague floated through my already addled brain.

I feared Lymes Disease. (Our county is close to Lyme, Connecticut, the place where Lymes Disease was first identified.) And I wondered continually if these mice carried ticks with the Lyme spirochete.

Then a friend mentioned that snakes gravitated toward areas where mice lived.

My hormonal imbalance and sleeplessness caused wakeful nightmares. I now had constant irrational fears that snakes were on the property.

One neighbor told me that the mice had invaded the block when an old shed had been torn down. "They just scattered everywhere!" she said.

Another neighbor, who also was trying to be helpful, told me, "Count the number of mice you see and multiply that number by 10." In the year since we had moved into the house, we had caught about 15 mice. I didn't even want to think about the possibility that she might be right.

New mothers always worry about their children, and I had more than my share of worries. Clearly, a new mother with hormonal imbalance and postpartum depression shouldn't have had to face a house full of frolicking mice—a house that seemed utterly beyond repair to boot. I wanted to move, but my husband was out of a regular job, and the short-term assignments hardly paid our bills. There was no way we could afford to fix the house anytime soon.

One day, after a year of living with this situation, an old kindergarten song started bouncing about in my brain: "The cat came back the very next day. We thought it was a-goner but the cat came back." So the song went.

After two days of "hearing" this song in my mind, I saw a small black cat appear at our son's windowsill. Obviously a stray, the cat was determined to join our little family, but we didn't encourage her, and after several days, the cat disappeared and was gone forever. We continued with our mouse problem.

Several months later, the song started again in my brain. "The cat came back the very next day. We thought it was a-goner but the cat came back." I couldn't get the song out of my mind.

Within a couple of days, another cat appeared. This one was an orange tabby, and once again, we tried to get rid of our annoying stray. But unlike her predecessor, this kitty was not going to take "no" for an answer. Whenever we opened a door or a window, she would rush past us into the house.

I told my husband that we were not keeping the cat. But every day she arrived, and whenever we opened the door, she would fly past us and up the stairs or into the kitchen. Repeatedly, we chased her down, lifted her, and tossed her out.

Then one day in the midst of this little battle, I remembered the song. I decided to let the cat stay.

The cat turned out to be a wonderful gift. We soon discovered that this cat, that we named Ralphina, was a major-league mouser. We would be lying in bed when we would suddenly hear a commotion downstairs. In the mornings, Ralphina would greet us with a little mouse in her mouth. It was as if the cavalry had come in and taken charge.

Within a month, the mice that had been plaguing us for a year had all disappeared. Our baby son could now crawl freely on the floor.

I've never really been a "cat person," but I ended up loving this cat. She was the best present God could have sent me.
In addition to being an excellent mouser, she is a perfectly trained
indoor-outdoors cat. I was thankful for this, since I had my son
to take care of first and foremost. But even better, Ralphina is
very gentle. She likes children and, all in all, is quite pleasant to
have around.

I will always think that God sent her to my house with
the specific instruction that she "not give up" so she could help
remove some of the petty annoyances that were overwhelming
me. After she arrived and gradually, but effectively, dispatched
the mice, I even started seeing the possibilities in our dream
house.

6

Angels Among Us

Do not forget to entertain strangers, for by so doing some people have entertained angels without knowing it.

— *Hebrews 13:2*

Abandoned Apricots

By Bonnie Compton Hanson
Santa Ana, California, United States

If an amusement park can be called the "happiest place on earth," a hospital ICU waiting room must surely be the saddest. And most terrifying. That's "ICU," as in "Intensive Care Unit." As in life and death.

By 11:30 a.m. on a sweltering Tuesday, June 23, 1992, I felt I had memorized every spot of the ICU waiting room in the Hemet, California, hospital. Ceiling, floor, walls, worn furniture. Plastic plants. Well-thumbed magazines. Plus all the other people waiting there with me. They included two women on a tour from Iowa whose friend suddenly became critically ill when their bus reached this quiet desert town. And another woman who was trying to run her family's business while her husband was dying from cancer and heart trouble. And had cancer herself. Still another woman, married 50 years, who for the past 20 years had been traveling with her husband everywhere he wanted to go—and all that time had really longed to settle down. Now at last her husband was ready to agree to her wishes—if he lived through the night. One woman's son had overdosed. Oh, so many needy ones to talk with, to pray with.

But, oh, Lord, who will minister to me—and to my breaking heart? For I, too, had a loved one behind those forbidding doors. Someone I could visit only 10 minutes out of each hour. Not knowing if each hour—or each minute—would be his last. My beloved husband, Don.

Just the Saturday before, though it seemed a million years ago now, we had driven the 90 miles from Orange County to Hemet for the day. The occasion was a big family get-together for the West Coast relatives to meet the Midwestern children and grandchildren of my 86-year-old father-in-law's new bride.

"Bring your trumpet and keyboard along, too," Dad told us. "I'll get out my sax and clarinet, and we'll have a little music after lunch to celebrate." But I fussed at Don all the way there, just as I had done the night before at an Angels' baseball game when he kept jumping up and twisting so ridiculously that I had demanded we leave early. Was he going to be a "pill" today, too?

Finally we were there meeting everyone. And when lunch was delayed, our little trio went ahead and entertained with some old-time favorites. At 3:00 p.m., we were ready to eat. Everyone rushed to get into line, hungry, laughing, and chattering away. Everyone except Don. He had simply disappeared.

When I finally found him, 15 minutes later, he was staggering out of the bathroom in the middle of a major heart attack. Ever since, we'd been here at the hospital—Don trying desperately to survive with 45 percent of his heart muscle destroyed—and me sitting here around the clock, longing and praying.

Don's folks came by to see him a couple of times each day, but they were busy with that houseful of out-of-town visitors. All my friends were 90 miles away. One of my sons was up in Northern California and another seriously ill with bronchitis. The third came down as often as he could, but he had to keep driving back to L.A. to work, a couple of hours' drive each way.

Other Christians tried to comfort me. The hospital chaplain stopped by. One pastor called from L.A. Dad Hanson's pastor visited.

When I called in to report Don's heart attack to his insurance company, the girl who answered the phone prayed with me right then and promised to have her whole church pray, too. Not to mention that concerned friends and relatives from all over the country kept the nearby pay phone ringing off the hook.

But I was still miserable: From guilt for not realizing that Don's "gyrations" the night before were simply attempts to shake off the pain of angina. From fear of a possible future without him. I felt so lonely, helpless, and utterly bereft.

"Dear Lord," I prayed, "I know this is impossible, but, oh, I would so like to have another Christian with me, to hug me and hold my hand and pray with me!" Then, sighing, I sank back into my misery.

About an hour later, the waiting room door pushed open. A young woman entered, looking around hesitantly. Her face glistened with perspiration, her hair was tousled, and her clothes were covered with a large apron—an apron full of orange stains. What in the world had brought her here in such a rush that she hadn't even taken off her apron? Someone's car wreck? Or some other sudden tragedy?

"E-Excuse me," she stammered, "but, uh, is anyone here waiting for a Don Hanson?"

"I-I'm Bonnie Hanson," I gasped. "But—?" She smiled shyly and held out her hand.

"Hi, I'm April. I've been sent to pray with you." Then she explained. "See, I live in Orange County. But I've been out here all week helping my mom can apricots. Just a while ago, my husband called me from home. He said prayer chains all over the county were praying for someone named Don Hanson who was in the hospital here in Hemet.

"'You're the only one I know who can help,' my husband said, 'because you're already in Hemet. Why don't you go to the hospital and see if you can pray with his family?'"

"So I dropped the apricots, told Mom where I was going, and jumped in the car. And here I am. Let's pray."

Then she took my hand, hugged me, and prayed with me.

Afterwards she said, "Well, better get back to my apricots."

Another hug, and she was gone.

I hadn't even asked her last name! But she left me filled with joy and peace. God had answered my prayer after all. Exactly the way I'd asked Him to! Even though I really didn't believe that He would! Through someone who never hesitated a moment when God asked her to do something that probably seemed totally off-the-wall and absurd—but she just went ahead and did it—gladly, joyfully, as naturally as breathing. Even if it meant abandoning her apricots—and wearing a stained apron out in public!

My beloved husband did survive and is now once more strong and full of life. How grateful we are for caring doctors, our loving Heavenly Father, our dear family, and all our Christian friends—even those we didn't know we had. Thank you, April!

The Dark Man

By Alaine Benard
Baton Rouge, Louisiana, United States

The Dark Man came to her aid right after her seventh birthday. While running down the hall, she had fallen across the furnace floor grate. Her Buster Brown sandals had somehow caught the metal and thrown her down, shredding her knee like rat trap cheese on a tin grater. Alone and not knowing what to do, the hurt child curled into a ball and wept while her body went into shock.

Her next cognizant thought was surprise at being lifted by a man with coffee-colored skin. She remembers hearing the whir of the ceiling fan and the way her thin blonde hair flew across her face and blocked her vision. The smell of some unnamed oil filled her nose, as she became aware that her tattered knee was completely numb. Happiness flooded her little soul at the disappearance of the burning pain. So grateful was she that she didn't realize she was standing on the grass in front of her beloved grandfather, Pappy. Squatting down, he was applying ointment and unrolling gauze, while gently soothing her with his soft words and kind ministrations.

Pappy carried her piggyback through the Louisiana breezes and cricket chirps. Then off to the Pac-a-Sac they went to get a treat. In the excitement and relief at the trauma's passing, she forgot about the Dark Man. She had, however, smelled a coconut smell all the way around the corner and to the store.

The Dark Man made his mysterious appearances off and on throughout her youth. While the gawky girl could put no face to her black knight, she instinctively knew he would find her each time she encountered a crisis.

Once at 12, while not paying attention, she walked into the path of an oncoming car. Standing frozen, like a deer trapped in the headlights, she waited for the impact. Then, with a blur of sound and time, she came back to herself on the opposite side of the street. As her heart beat furiously, she looked everywhere for her secret friend. She'd run circles around each azalea bush in search of him. Where could he have gone? The girl whispered her "thank-you's" into the dusk and prayed he'd heard. The incident faded as her best friend pulled her away to their clubhouse and waiting Barbie dolls.

College days came and brought with them temptations of all sorts—many in which the woman indulged. Yet, whenever terror entered her life, usually brought on by those very same temptations, her protector was there reaching out. Flashes of his smooth white palms, so in contrast with his beadle nut skin, danced across her mind.

At the age of independence, his presence began to wear on her nerves. Why on earth would she need the likes of this shadow man? He skulked around, spied on her, and often irritated her with his overprotective watchfulness. She no longer wanted a mentor, a knight. She wanted life without interference from him, or anyone else for that matter.

For the next several years, the Dark Man vanished. The only times he came to her were in brief glimpses in her dreams. She would wake with misty remnant knowledge of her head resting upon his shoulder, soaking up the comfort of him. Then, just as quickly, she'd drift back into chenille wrapped sleep.

She'd be drying her hair, daydreaming, or zooming around town in her old Volkswagen Bug when she'd catch his unique aroma. "Sandalwood Oil" is what she had named it in her head.

Upon "feeling him," she would concentrate with all her might and try to bring him to her. Other than the rare dream snippet, he never fully materialized.

Marriage and maturity took the place of her freewheeling lifestyle, and she soon forgot about him altogether. She had a husband, her own household, and a career to manage; she needed nothing else. Her adult, independent life was ahead of her. She let go of childhood things and concentrated on making the most of her real life. She had everything she needed right in front of her. Or so she thought.

****

The Dark Man found his childhood charge when she returned to the church of her youth. On the Christmas Eve of her 30th year, he brought the woman a gift sent straight from God. He delivered the message that his friend, the infertile woman who had worn Buster Brown sandals so many years ago, would bear a son in nine months time. He hadn't abandoned her after all.

She thanked him profusely through tears and hugs. He promised to be with her through the upcoming difficult labor and delivery. Twenty-six hours of natural childbirth brought forth a perfect baby boy to the woman and her husband.

Stressed and exhausted, she slept holding the child to her breast, but not before she felt the Dark Man kiss both of their brows. The smell—his scent—sent her off into languid slumber.

Through the remainder of her years, she never again hid from the Dark Man—for she now knew with certainty that he had never left her. And he never would. They formed a partnership and accomplished many works together.

The middle-aged woman came to understand that her son had not been the first miraculous gift sent to her from Heaven. The Dark Man had been with her since birth—a gift from God. Through the entirety of her life, he had guided, protected, and prayed for her.

The Dark man is her personal guardian angel—the epitome of faithfulness and perseverance, sent to walk beside her each day.

And how my heart lifts each time I smell the mysterious coconut scent.

I Just Want to See My Babies

By Jozette Aaron
Oshawa, Ontario, Canada

It was a balmy summer's eve, and I was in the middle of my shift when Katie came in. She was uncomfortable with her contractions and asking for pain medication. Katie was in active labor with twins. She had delivered her first child after only a few hours of labor, so it was necessary to get control of this delivery as soon as possible.

"Please...please help me. I want to push—" she said as the force of her next contraction hit her.

"Pant, Katie—" I said as I pulled the emergency bell for extra help with her admission.

"Maybe you should examine her—see how much time we have," one of my co-workers suggested.

We managed to get Katie changed into a hospital gown, her husband arriving just as I was preparing to examine her.

"Is she ready to deliver?" he asked as he dropped her suitcase and pillows into the nearby rocking chair.

Before I could answer, another contraction gripped Katie in its powerful embrace.

"I want to push!" Katie yelled, her face suffusing with color, eyes wild with fright.

"No pushing, Katie. Look at me—that's it—keep your eyes here." I instructed her, using two of my fingers to point to my eyes.

"Now, pant like a puppy. Huh-huh-huh. That's it—good. Is the contraction over?" I asked her as she let go of a last whoosh of breath.

"Yes," she answered feebly. "Please…it hurts—Craig? Where's Craig?" she asked, hysteria coating her words as she craned her neck to look for her husband.

"I'm right here, Baby…right here," Craig reassured her, stepping into her line of vision and reaching for her hand.

"How much longer is it going to be?" he asked me as I finished examining her and tidying her bed sheets.

"Not long," I reassured him. I applied the fetal monitor to assess the twins' heart rates and how they were coping with the contractions. I gave Katie a reassuring pat on her shoulder and left the room to call her obstetrician.

"Is Dr. Jefferson in the building?" I asked the secretary as I rounded the desk at the nurse's station. "Please see if you can find him for me."

"Right away," was all she said, reading the urgency in my voice.

Dr. Jefferson answered his page a short time later, and I gave him a report on his patient.

"I'll be up to see Katie in a minute."

When Dr. Jefferson arrived, I was coaching Katie through another contraction, this one seemingly more distressing than the others. He waited patiently, palpating her abdomen, until the contraction ebbed. He examined her again and then spoke with both Katie and Craig about how their babies would be born.

"The first baby is in a transverse lie position. By this, I mean that the baby is lying sideways. The reason why you are feeling the urge to push is because the amniotic sac is bulging, putting pressure on your cervix, which is only dilated at 4 centimeters. You will need a cesarean section to deliver these babies. You will be given an epidural so you can see your babies when they're born. Craig can be with you in the OR. Any questions?"

"When can I get something for this pain?" Katie inquired, clearly exhausted by her labor.

"I'll see what the anesthetist is doing and if we can get you into the OR now, and then you can have your epidural. Just try to get through a couple more contractions, OK?"

Katie only shook her head...whimpering as another contraction hit her. Craig held her hand and helped her with her breathing. I went to gather the things needed to prep Katie for surgery.

"Make sure the pediatrician and the respiratory tech are there. I am going to call the OR. Once I arrange a time for her, I'll be back to see her. If those babies show signs that they aren't coping with the contractions, page me stat!" Dr. Jefferson said as he headed for the surgical lounge.

"Will do," I said as I headed off to make the necessary arrangements.

I checked on Katie several times during the following 20 minutes, and it was on the last check that I noticed a change in the fetal hearts and called Dr. Jefferson as instructed. He arrived almost immediately and studied the monitor tracing before speaking.

"She can't wait any longer. I'm bumping this to a stat c-section!" Dr. Jefferson said. "Get her down now, and I'll meet you there. Katie, I'll see you soon OK? Don't worry. Everything will be all right," he said to the patient before leaving the room.

"Are my babies all right?" Katie asked, fear and pain evident in her voice. Craig looked to me for reassurance as I rang the bell for assistance.

"Follow us to the OR, Craig. I'll show you where to change, OK? You were planning on going in with her, right?"

Nodding his head, Craig followed as we took Katie to the service elevators. The elevator had been placed on standby so we didn't have to wait. The doors slid closed, and suddenly there was silence.

"How old is the baby at home?" I asked, wanting to break the silence and keep them focused on the positive.

"She's two years old—" Katie answered just as another contraction seized her.

"Look at me Katie. Come on—pant—*pant!*" I instructed her, including Craig in the lesson.

"That's it…good. Craig, keep her focused and help her with her breathing," I told him as the doors opened and we emerged in the surgical suite holding area. I directed Craig to the changing area and told him to be seated once he was changed.

"Someone will come for you once we get Katie's epidural in."

He looked at me and then his wife, bending to give her a quick kiss before letting go of her hand and walking in the opposite direction.

Katie was taken to OR six and transferred to the surgical table. The anesthetist told Katie about the procedure as I listened to the fetal hearts. Both babies were doing fine—it was Katie I was concerned with. She looked a little paler, and she was a little short of breath.

"Slow that breathing down, Katie. You're going to hyperventilate. When you're not having a contraction, let your breaths come slowly…naturally."

The epidural insertion was completed just as Dr. Jefferson entered the OR. Katie was repositioned on the table, and her abdomen was scrubbed with an antibacterial soap and then painted with an iodine solution before the sterile drapes were applied.

I called out to the main desk for Craig to be escorted into the OR, and he arrived just as the first incision was made. He was seated near the head of the table, his view of the procedure hidden by the surgical sheets. I peeked at Katie to see if she was comfortable and saw a slightly grayish-blue tinge to her face that worried me. I looked up to see the anesthetist looking at me with concern on his face, as well.

Katie's daughters were born less than five minutes after the surgery began. They were healthy, squalling, chubby-faced moppets with tufts of curly auburn hair.

After cleaning up the babies and carefully placing the correct identification on them and their mother, I wrapped them warmly and took them, one at a time, to meet their parents.

Craig held the first one, and when I brought over the other, I noticed that Katie had drifted off, that gray-blue tinge still evident. I placed the baby in her father's arms and went to finish my charting.

"Please take the babies to the Neonatal Intensive Unit (NICU)," the pediatrician ordered. "I will be able to examine them more thoroughly there."

Dr. Jefferson asked that Craig accompany his daughters and me. "Katie will be in recovery shortly. You can see her when she gets to her room. Congratulations...*Dad,*" he said to Craig.

I placed the twins in an isolette for transport to the NICU, and after thanking the OR nurses for their assistance, took father and daughters from the room. As the door closed, I could hear the cardiac monitor begin to alarm and a stifled flurry of activity. I got that same queasy feeling as I rolled the isolette to the elevator.

"Grab your clothes and meet me at the elevators. I'll wait for you there. It'll be easier for you to change upstairs, OK?"

Craig nodded and went to collect his belongings, returning just as the elevator door slid open. We arrived at the NICU, and the babies were turned over to the nursery nurses. I gave my report and shook hands with Craig.

"I'll see you guys tomorrow, OK? Congratulations…again."

"Thanks. I appreciate all you did for me and Katie," Craig said as he followed his daughters to the admission area of the NICU. I retraced my steps and took the elevators to the labor and delivery unit. It was time to go home.

By the time I changed from my scrubs and got ready to go, a call came through from Dr. Jefferson, wanting to know what the census was before deciding to leave the hospital.

"Let me talk to him a minute," I told the secretary as she ended her conversation.

I grabbed the phone and was able to get through before Dr. Jefferson hung up.

"How's Katie? I heard the monitors going off. Is she OK?"

"She's fine—just a positional thing, that's all. She's in recovery right now."

"Thanks, Dr. Jefferson," I said as I hung up the phone and left for home.

I had a hard time sleeping that night. Images of chubby-pink cheeks on a pale-gray face followed me through my dreams. I woke the next morning tired and still heavyhearted.

Arriving at work, I immediately went to check on the twins. As I approached the NICU, Katie was being rolled on a stretcher to the nursery. I quickened my steps to find out what the problem was.

"She's going up to the Intensive Care Unit," I was told when I asked why Katie was on a stretcher.

"Please—I just want to see my babies," Katie cried.

"The nurses are going to bring the babies over to you because the stretcher won't fit in the NICU, OK? You'll be able to see them and touch them," I reassured Katie.

Looking at her, I saw no improvement in her color and went to talk with her nurse.

"She has something going on with her, and Dr. Jefferson wants her monitored closely. The postpartum area is too busy, so we're sending her upstairs. She started crying when she was told that she would have to wait a couple of days before she could hold the babies, so we brought her by on our way upstairs. She can at least *see* them and touch their little hands."

I watched as Katie reached for her daughter's hand...tiny fingers curling around one bigger one...a thumb caressing a tiny wrist. The visit was brief, and all too soon, Katie was wheeled, crying, towards the elevator. As she passed by, I leaned over her and, stroking her hair away from her sweat-dampened forehead, told her that she would see them again as soon as she got better. I gave her a gentle hug and watched as she was wheeled down the corridor to the elevators at the far end. The morning sun cast a swirling pinkish-yellow haze around the stretcher, and again, my feelings of trepidation returned.

For the remainder of the shift, I was kept busy with other patients, other babies. On my way home, I stopped in the nursery to see the twins. Craig was there with his other daughter, another moppet with long blond curls. She was dressed in pink frills, lacy socks, and white leather shoes. She was standing on tiptoes trying to see her sisters while hanging onto her daddy's pants. Craig stooped to pick her up just as I approached.

I talked with them for a few minutes and asked after Katie.

"She's asleep right now, so I thought I'd bring Abby to see her sisters," Craig informed me.

After a few more minutes, I said goodnight and made my way home.

The evening was humid and the sun a golden orange. I walked home, needing the extra long time to deal with my feelings. I chided myself for getting personally involved—something we are taught *not* to do, but something that happens from time to time.

I said a prayer for this little family that night. I wanted everything to be OK for them. I wanted that queasy feeling that gripped me since meeting Katie and Craig to let go.

I arrived at work the next morning, and all eyes were on me. Looking down at my uniform in case I hadn't remembered to put my scrubs on, I asked why I was being scrutinized. My boss walked over to me, and as the words left her mouth, my ears pounded, my heart broke, and I started to cry.

Katie had died during the night—from undiagnosed cardiomyopathy. I thought of Craig and his three daughters, two of whom would never know their mother's love.

I thought about the last time I saw Katie, and I was so glad that I could comfort her and be there for her in what became her last hours.

Anne's Song

By Vanessa K. Mullins
Milan, Michigan, United States

I met Anne about 10 years ago when she started working for the same company that I worked for. At first glance, I knew I wouldn't like her. She was too perfect: blonde hair, beautiful smile, cute figure—the kind of woman you just know is going to be "witchy," to put it nicely.

After a while, Anne was promoted to a management position similar to mine. We attended meetings together, and afterwards, we would go someplace to talk. The more I got to know her, the more I realized my first impression had been so very wrong. She was very friendly and very full of life. Anne became the first woman friend I ever had.

Eventually both of us were laid off from our jobs, and Anne ended up moving in one direction, while I moved 200 miles in the other. Still, whenever we would see each other, it was like we had never been apart. When it was time to leave, we both cried like babies.

Over the years, Anne and I have both experienced difficulties that were hard for us to get through on our own. Then we've talked with each other and found that the other has had the same experience at some point earlier in her life. This makes it easier to know what to say and how to get through the bad times and into the good.

When I need someone to talk to, or cry to, or just listen to me complain, I call Anne. She's always there for me. It doesn't matter what it is, or even what time it is—Anne gives me a safe place to go for comfort.

She helped me through one of the toughest times in my life. She was there for me—angry when I was angry, hurt when I was hurt—and eventually, she was happy for me when I finally got it all back together. Her friendship never wavered. She was my strength when I had none.

Years later, when I found out Anne was diagnosed with cancer, I realized that she was almost a physical part of me. I knew that if I lost her, it would be like losing a piece of myself. I knew that if something happened to her, I would never be the same. Thank God, she beat it. To this day, I thank God that I still have Anne in my life.

Through the years of friendship, we have helped each other through divorce, death, new marriages, and the births of our children. These experiences have brought us closer emotionally, even though physically we are further apart.

It is through one of these hardships that Anne and I learned just how very connected we are.

Anne's mother passed away after a lengthy illness. I had never met her mom and didn't know much about her except that she had been sick for a while.

That night, I had a dream with a beautiful young lady in it who told me her name was Kathleen and that she was Anne's mother. She was lovely and very happy in my dream. I had never met Anne's mom and she had never really told me too much about her, much less given her name. When I woke the next morning, I forgot about the dream—until a few days later.

The next night, I had a very vivid dream that stuck with me throughout the entire day. In the dream, I was in the water, and Anne came floating by on her way to Pontiac, Michigan. I told her she should get a boat. Then I awoke. All day I thought about this dream—I couldn't get it off my mind.

I called Anne to see how she was doing. To cheer her up a little bit, I told her I had a silly dream about her. I related the dream to her. She got quiet for a moment and then told me why.

Anne told me that her mother's favorite song was "If I Had a Boat" from a CD by Lyle Lovett called "Pontiac." Anne had been thinking about her mother and playing this song over and over the day before. Incidentally, I am not a country music fan. I had never heard of either the song or the title of the CD. We both had chills.

I then asked her what her mom's name was. She told me "Kathy."

Chills ran through me again when I remembered the dream with the woman—Kathleen. I told Anne about that dream.

Somehow, in some way, both Anne and I believe that her mother came through my dreams to let Anne know she was all right now—no longer in pain—and that she was happy.

Both Anne and I feel a spiritual connection to each other that neither time nor distance can break. We always know when the other needs us, and we are always there for each other.

7

His Perfect Timing

There is a time for everything,
and a season for every activity under heaven:
— Ecclesiastes 3:1

Wait A While

By Julie Bonn Heath
Port Orchard, Washington, United States

When I was young, my dad often said that God always answers us when we pray—whether it was a matter of something small like asking how to spend $5.00 or something larger like choosing between two colleges.

"God always answers," Dad would say. "He answers three different ways."

"But He's not answering me," I would reply, frowning at my dad and wondering what he heard that I could not.

There'd been no voice from the sky, my Bible had not given me guidance on the subject—at least not where I looked, and there were no obvious open doors anywhere around me. Why was God so silent sometimes? Here I was, as a child and a young adult, making some serious, life-changing decisions. All I needed was for God to point me in the right direction.

Should I take that part-time job after school that I think I might not like, just because nothing else has come along? And what about college? Wasn't it important that I choose the right one? And if so, why was God being so quiet about the subject?

I remember being very frustrated about many decisions I had to make, because it seemed that God was so silent about what I should do.

And yet, my dad's words always echoed in my head, "God always answers. His answers are 'yes,' 'no,' or 'wait a while.'"

So, growing up, if His answers were unclear, I would take it to mean that I was to wait awhile. I did, and things always worked out.

You would think an important childhood lesson such as this would stick in my head and my heart as an adult. You would think that I would remember. But I forgot, and God had to teach me again.

In my grown-up family, my husband is disabled and cares for our children; I am the breadwinner. For many years, I have become increasingly frustrated about my job situation. We live in a rural area, own our home on two acres, and have no desire to move. But the jobs in our area pay very little, and I have been unable to find a local job that pays enough to support the family. As it is, I commute two hours each way to work, across the water where the pay is better. On Friday nights and the nights before a holiday, it takes me three to three and a half hours to get home.

As many times as we've considered it, relocating is not an option, as my husband needs to be near his extended family for support.

No one can claim that I haven't done more than my share of looking for jobs in our home area. I could probably go down in history books as the job searcher who has been looking the longest. I certainly know that when I tell people how long I have been looking, they are amazed and then concerned. I'm sure they are wondering what is wrong with me and why I can't obtain employment where I need to.

I continue to scour the classified ads. I send out resumes for positions, many that I am overqualified for, and I interview when the opportunity arises. But have I been offered a job around home in the past five years? No.

"This is silly," I tell myself. "Why can't I get a job here, even in sales? I am qualified enough, capable enough, and so motivated to stay here in this area that they would definitely have a long-term employee on their hands."

But invariably I hear, "I'm sorry. You were a close second." Or most of the time, I hear nothing at all.

Talk about an ego blower! Is this a lesson in humility? OK, I've learned it. I am sure eating humble pie after searching locally for so many years with no results.

Now I'm on board with the other people I've talked to about this particular journey. What in the world is the matter with me?

Things just get worse. I get even more frustrated with my current job across the water and the commute. I have a third baby, and after a couple months of leave, am away from him 13 hours a day. The older two kids start having academic problems.

"What greater sign is there that my children need me home more?" I cry. "Don't you see that, God? I can't imagine You not seeing the need for me to be home more!"

This is not to mention that my husband's medical problems mean that several times during the year, he is unable to care for the kids, and I stay home from work to do so. If there ever is a family that needs their mommy, it is mine.

I start having my own medical problems—several different ones, but all related to stress. I am diagnosed with Raynoud's disease, attacks of which are triggered by stress. I hold my head in pain, because I am having bad muscle tension headaches, obviously related to stress (and the commute). I start feeling depressed and cannot seem to pull myself out of the slump.

Every Sunday night when I rock my one-year-old to sleep, I cry. I know that I will not see him the next morning, and after having all weekend with him, it is an unbearable thought. And I continue to cry, "Why Lord? Why? I don't understand! Why aren't You hearing me? I cannot believe that You think it is the best thing for me to be gone so long every day!"

Work gets harder now. Even my co-workers are discussing leaving the organization, as we have an extremely difficult boss and a very unorganized environment to work in. Every day there are irritations and downright angry moments. Every day there is hurt and frustration and thoughts of "Why am I here?" and "I can't do this anymore."

It is here, at wit's end, that I finally grasp for some help. I am desperate. I am inches away from walking into work the next day and quitting on the spot without having another job and benefits for my family. I just cannot handle any more. There is no way on this earth that I can do this anymore. Nothing has changed, in spite of my pleas. God has not heard me. Or, I reason, He doesn't care. I am on my own, and in spite of using all the resources that I can think of, nothing has changed.

I log on to the computer that night to research at-home work opportunities. Having always hoped a little in my heart that my writing career would take off and either give us some extra income or allow me to eventually stay at home, I decide to start researching how I can get some of my articles and stories published. This I am doing, of course, with myself at the helm of my ship. For it does not occur to me that, by His grace, I am truly only a crewmember.

But God knows that I am at my wit's end this night. I post to my Christian Internet group that I desperately need a length of rope, as mine has seriously run out. I cry as I type. I pour my heart out to these sisters in Christ whom I have never met, and afterwards, I begin to research publication possibilities on the Internet.

It is God who makes moves that night. God who moves mountains, not to get me a local job, but to bring me peace, draw me back into His arms, and begin His work. I find a site that features moms who write professionally. Through a list of perhaps one hundred names, I choose a few to email and ask for publishing advice.

Because I am so desperate, I also pour my heart into these emails, telling them about my commute and my children and my desire to be with them more; therefore, I need to publish my work and do they have any advice to offer?

When I wrap up my computer work that night, I realize something. Many of the woman authors on the site had talked about how close they were to God or how they are writing for Him. And I realize that I am not walking very close to God at all. I realize that I have been trying to navigate my own boat, because I don't have the time or patience to fully trust Him with it.

I realize that I am being disobedient, because I have not been spending personal devotional and prayer time with Him. I can certainly cry and pray for release from my pains. But who am I to ask things of Him when I am not giving Him what He asks of me in the first place?

The next Sunday at church, when our music minister prays, he says, "Help us to remember, Lord, that we should not be asking how we are going to handle the next day or week, but how YOU are going to handle it."

His words strike me and echo in my head. I have not given this to God. I have refused to accept the circumstances He has given me. I have not trusted God with taking care of my struggle. I am still not casting my cares upon Him. For, although I pray in my anguish to Him, I have not truly let it go, or I would be at peace knowing He is in control. Instead, I am fighting God with all my might. And I have lost.

God and I work things out. I understand now that the job and the commute are the least of His concerns. He's been wondering where His daughter has gone. He is waiting patiently for my return. He hadn't walked away; it was me. When I give it all to Him, no matter what the cost, I feel incredible peace. He has given me my length of "rope" when I was swinging with only inches left.

Immediately, I begin my quiet time and prayer time with Him every morning on the ferry. And my prayers change. All of a sudden, I find myself praying not, "Lord, please get me a job close to home," but "Lord, I accept Your will for me, which obviously *is* this current job right now, and I trust You. I also trust that You love my family just as much as I do and will take care of them. Give me patience and show me the way You want me to go."

My priorities have shifted. I want His will for me, whatever that is, because I know that it is for the best—even if I do not understand it.

I receive a couple of responses to my email publishing inquiries. One lady, Karon, is extremely understanding and gives me some good advice. Underneath her signature on the email is a link to her website, and I click on it to check out her books.

Lo and behold, the second book down is titled, *You're Late Again, Lord! The Impatient Woman's Guide to God's Timing.** Needless to say, I am shocked. This sounds like something I really need. God has taken me from a search engine requesting sites for writers, to a site featuring moms as writers, to choosing this woman's name out of a hundred others, to emailing her publishing questions (she doesn't know God had her keep her email address current just for me), to clicking a link to her website, and finally, to this book. I order the book, email my thanks (and amazement) to her, and eagerly wait for its arrival.

I wish I could say that I will never struggle again. God is teaching me, through this book, "that I am in a waiting room right now." It is very painful to be in this waiting room, but I am there to draw close to Him, to grow, and to eventually share that with others. I am learning that while I wait, I am to be productive, not frustrated. And I am to know that He is there with me.

I do not understand my purpose here yet, but I trust Him. I do not know what the future holds, but I sure know who is in charge of it.

I am still having major frustrations at work. In fact, they have increased. More challenges come every day. I still miss my children terribly when I am gone. I am still having some medical problems, although the depression is gone, and this has brought on some doubt. "How can this be God's will when there is so much pain involved?"

Then He gently brings Job to my thoughts. And I am reminded that we are tested in spite of our faith—that we are asked to bear trials for the purpose of growth or for the purpose of helping others. Job survived the ultimate testing with God at his side. I hope that I can one day say the same.

Karon's book was, and still is, a great encouragement. The steps she has been through in her waiting periods are the same steps that I am going through. It is like having a best friend to hold my hand—one who has "been there." From her book, I have adopted what I need to focus on while waiting, and I wrote those things down and keep them posted in my car to remind me as I am commuting:

"Accept the circumstances; Acknowledge Him and Accomplish the daily tasks."

"As you move nearer to the Lord," Karon says, *"all the noise around you will begin to make sense or it will not matter anymore."*

A few days ago, when my parent's asked how work was going, I responded with, "It's not my battle anymore."

What I should have told them was, "God's answer was, 'Wait a while.'"

You're Late Again, Lord! The Impatient Woman's Guide to God's Timing, by Karon Phillips Goodman, Barbour Books ©2002. Quotes and references used with permission.

Angel Bus Intuition

By Karla Jensen
Beaver Dam, Wisconsin, United States

In my understanding of faith, I believe that God allowed His omnipotent timing to intervene in my life so that I could be in the right place at the right time.

My presence at a new job—one I never intended to take—not only allowed my boss and his family time away from the office to deal with a family health crisis, but also granted me a time to experience the most profound faith in action. I personally witnessed how God touches lives when tragedy strikes and random suffering enters. This is how my story evolved.

As the owner of a freelance advertising agency, I occasionally perused the want ads hoping to spy a unique opportunity that might fit into my creative endeavors, but only on a part-time basis.

However, after accepting an offer of a full time job, I thought I had discovered my career path for the next decade. The 15-minute commute worked well for my schedule, and I received Fridays off, which I spent with my husband. For nearly a year, I continued my freelance agency work for a limited number of clients without searching the newspaper ads. I enjoyed my current full-time job and had just enough side projects to keep me happy.

But one Sunday afternoon, I discovered myself unusually drawn to the classified section. For months, I had not even glanced at the employment ads. In this particular Sunday paper, there appeared a job for a writer and marketing director of a new national niche magazine. *Something right up my alley,* I told myself.

Although I excelled in radio and television advertising, I had never imagined myself wishing to pursue a career in the magazine publishing industry or in print media of any kind. I had always envisioned a more frustrated me in the print field, since broadcast media seemed so much more active than passive.

In fact, *why did I even show an interest in this job at all,* I wondered, since I felt thoroughly satisfied with where life had led me these past 12 months? So what if the office for the magazine was less than five blocks from my house.

Still, I wondered if I might be better off working in the same town I lived in, so I challenged myself to drop off a resume at the magazine office, even though weeks had passed since I spotted that first ad. Certainly, by now, I reasoned, the magazine would have found a qualified professional to accept the plum job.

I dropped by the office one windy winter day and met Bill and Nola Connor, never imagining how intimately I would come to know them in just a few short weeks.

Bill later reviewed my resume, and then called me at home to set an appointment to visit with him and his wife about their new endeavor. *Private Coach Enthusiast Magazine* featured historical articles about buses and converted motor homes and travel and motorhome amenities.

I knew as much about buses as I did about aerospace engineering. How could my knowledge and talents fit into such an odd niche? I wondered. Then I reminded myself that my top advertising agency client had been Sundstrand Aerospace, and I still knew squat about that industry. So what the heck! Something or someone urged me gently into the private coach industry.

I resigned from my other job two weeks before my start at *Private Coach,* wondering if my head was screwed on straight or if I had just given up a wonderful opportunity that could have led me down the path of product development and future managerial successes.

As I proudly but nervously stepped into the three-room office on Main Street in Dell Rapids, South Dakota, shocking news met my ears. My boss and his wife had just received the devastating news that Bill's son, Jaran, suffered from two inoperable brain tumors. They sped off immediately to spend the next week or more at the Mayo Clinic in Rochester, Minnesota.

They left their budding business in the confident and capable hands of me, someone who knew little or nothing about the industry that I would spend the next three years getting acquainted with.

In retrospect, had I not been available to "watch the store" for the Connors, their stress level surely would have been heightened and they may have felt obligated to leave one of them behind to continue their business.

In God's timing, I appeared when I was most needed so their family could unite to face the uncertain diagnosis of their son together. Bill certainly needed his wife's steadfast faith to deal with the hardships that were to come. If I hadn't been led to the Sunday paper weeks earlier, God's plan could not have fallen into place so precisely.

Until this time, I had never had the opportunity to work with someone who struggled daily with the suffering life, and possible death, of a family member. As Bill and I worked closely together to fulfill Bill's dream of debuting a national magazine, the atmosphere continued to be tainted by preoccupation with his son's health. Simultaneously, I felt a nagging intuition that something greater would be accomplished in this office. I felt it so strongly that I snagged a sheet of paper and hand wrote myself a note, dated it, and would later return to read what God had fulfilled.

What may have been Bill's dream of publishing a topnotch, coffee table-style book about buses, bus history, and converted coaches took on a new dimension after he spent much of his time accompanying his son to cancer treatments, radiation therapy, and MRIs.

Having witnessed plenty of sick children with stressed parents at the Mayo Clinic, Bill believed all families could be better off if they didn't have to worry about the long distance transportation necessary in situations where children may be critically ill. Bill utilized his own motorhome, which happened to be a converted GM bus, to transport Jaran to appointments and follow-up treatments. With home-like amenities—a bedroom, couch, TV, bathroom, galley, etc.—it took Jaran's mind off his life-threatening illness when he was able to enjoy the comforts of a motorhome, if even for a moment.

Since our new magazine catered to and included folks with converted coaches (similar to motorhomes), Bill accepted God's guidance in redirecting the focus of our publication. He founded Angel Bus, a non-profit organization that provides free transportation to children with life-threatening illnesses. Angel Bus sought volunteers from within the already established audience of magazine subscribers who presently owned a motorhome or showed interest in possibly purchasing one in the future. Angel Bus suddenly discovered a whole host of generous people whose unconditional love allowed miracles to be accomplished across the United States.

Now, after more than two years of completed missions, Angel Bus provides hope for families frustrated by too many bills and not enough resources. As God planned, I accepted the position as one of the first Angel Bus mission coordinators and worked with a fantastic group of caring individuals that gave back to society in a way that only God could have intended.

Although I never met many of the volunteer drivers face to face, I always felt a very close bond with drivers who altered schedules, footed fuel costs, and generally went far out of their way to help other human beings in need.

After three years of working with Private Coach and Angel Bus, I resigned my position when my spouse accepted a call to become pastor of a larger church in another state and we relocated. But I still cherish every moment I worked with Angel Bus, because our staff truly carried out the work of God. My work made a difference, and so did the work of all the folks who helped complete so many of the missions we accomplished.

From families who wished to see their children in hospice die at home, to infants separated from their parents by car accidents, Angel Bus answered random acts of suffering with random acts of kindness.

I recently turned to the back of my calendar from three years ago and withdrew the handwritten note I penned out of nagging intuition. Angel Bus became the organization that was yet unnamed in my notes, but completely and most certainly conceived by God.

The Right Place at the Right Time

By Alberta "Berta" Beversdorf
Port Richey, Florida, United States

His reliable and relatively new car, a 2001 Montero, was not starting.

Tossing his books onto the passenger seat, Bob sat behind the wheel. He had to get to his classes in Clearwater, but the car wasn't cooperating.

He turned on the headlight switch. Yes, the lights worked, so his battery was probably OK. Next he tried the key and the lights to see if they dimmed, which meant the starter was getting current. Sure enough, the battery seemed fine.

The SUV had been his pride and joy. He had worked hard and saved hard to be able to buy it. He wanted something sporty, but reliable and comfortable. Now he wondered, *What can I do?*

It was 8:00 a.m. on June 4, and he was upset and puzzled. Shaking his head as if to clear away the confusion, he prepared to raise the hood.

Then hearing the distinct sounds of a car starting up nearby, he remembered that Gus and Joe from down the street also attended the same college. Running up to Joe's car, Bob waved his hands. But Joe put his VW in gear and edged away from the curb.

"Joe! Gus!" The brake lights came on, the car eased over to the curb and parked.

Thank God! Bob thought.

"What's happenin'?" asked Gus. "Do ya need a jump or push?"

"No, thanks, it has a new battery, but for some reason it won't start!" Bob answered.

"If you're goin' to school, ya can ride with us," offered Joe.

"Yeah, great. Wait a second, and I'll get my bag." Bob was relieved, punched the air lightly, and went for his bag with a grin on his face. With his book bag slung over his shoulder, he gladly slid into Joe's back seat.

"Thanks, guys!" he said. He felt lucky to have such good friends.

Gus and Joe were going to anatomy class, and Bob was going to a biology course in the same building. Needing to do some research, Gus had decided to go in early and, of course, Joe drove him and planned to study for his test. Even though they had classes at the same campus, Bob was on a different schedule. It was a fortunate coincidence that they all were going at the same time.

Twenty minutes later, as they drove south on Highway 19 in New Port Richey, Joe muttered, "Ohmygod!" and slammed on his brakes.

A woman, who appeared to be in her 80's, was sprawled in the road. The car ahead of them had screeched to a halt.

Joe placed his car at an angle across the lane to protect the victim.

All three young men jumped out to assist the woman. Joe bent over and told her to keep still. Gently, he and Gus checked her over. She moaned and rolled her head back and forth. Straining to sit up, but unable to accomplish it, the lady finally relaxed back on the pavement.

The driver of the car that struck her was wringing her hands, crying openly, and grieving—she thought the worst had happened. Bob went to her, dialing 9-1-1 at the same time. He tried to calm the driver, then directed the traffic to go around the lane with the accident.

Soon the ambulance arrived and then a state trooper. Moments later a newspaper reporter came. As the facts became clearer, it was evident the pedestrian was "lucky." The driver who struck her was driving slowly due to rush-hour traffic.

Highway 19 is a divided main road that runs from north to south and parallels the Gulf of Mexico. It already had a terrible reputation for its high number of accidents. Especially sad is the number of pedestrian injuries and fatalities. This notorious Highway 19 was much dreaded by elder drivers, and many cars carried the bumper sticker sentiment: "Pray for me. I drive on US 19." Some drivers tended to drive erratically, shooting in and out of lanes and trying to advance on the busy highway.

In a confused state of mind, the woman had stepped out right into the stream of traffic! At any other time of day, she'd probably have been killed in a high-speed collision. It was a miracle she was not badly injured.

Gus and Joe took excellent care of her. They kept her safe and calm. Joe kept pressure on a bleeding wound, and Gus kept reassuring her.

Thanks to Bob's car problems, the three med-students had arrived just in time. Five seconds sooner would have put them ahead of the accident. The coincidence was remarkable!

That evening, Gus commented to Joe and Bob that God must have intervened somehow to put them in the right place at the right time. Both agreed, solemnly nodding.

Then Joe wondered, "Have you fixed your car?"

Bob replied, "No, I have no clue what is wrong."

"Well, let's see," suggested Joe.

Bob sat in the driver's seat and turned the key. It started up immediately!

God's hand was certainly steering them that day. They arrived in time to protect the pedestrian, an elderly lady who was wandering the streets in confusion. She had no purse or other identification and was desperately in need of medical attention. She got the care she needed, and now she also has three new friends who promised to look in on her and make sure she eats appropriately and takes her medications.

This encounter impacted Bob's life and direction. With a new commitment and strength, he is pursuing his dream of becoming of a doctor. He even feels directed to learn the specialty known as gerontology; he wants to know about elders and their special needs. Bob feels the nudge was in answer to his hesitation and doubts about his profession and choosing a specialty.

God works in mysterious ways—we know He performs His wonders in our lives every day. We just don't always realize how strong the influence is!

Was it God's touch on Bob's car engine? Bob's car has been reliable ever since!

Authors note: In the two-week period following the submission of this story, there were two separate fatal accidents near the same intersection where the "lucky" lady was struck.

A Gentle Nudge

By Gwen Morrison
Lawrenceville, Georgia, United States

Let me begin by saying that I don't believe in coincidences. I think that everything in life happens for a reason. Having said that, the story I am about to tell will show how God's hand was on my shoulder recently—nudging me—and I am so grateful to have listened to that gentle nudge.

I can't even remember where I found the advertisement. It was a call for submissions to an anthology—and it drew me in from the first sentence. *Forget Me Knots...from the Front Porch* is the title of the book. As I read further, I knew I had to write to this editor. "Where would we be without our memories?" it read. They were looking for stories about childhood memories—the ones that bring back those days long past when your life was different—when you were a child. They wanted stories that brought back the emotions of our youth—the tears, the laughter, and even the pain. I was so excited—wanting so badly to be included in this book.

I have memories. Surely I can come up with one that might interest other people.

I didn't know it at the time, but that was God's first little nudge. He was telling me to write a story. He didn't tell me what story—just write it.

I sat down at the computer screen and paused. What could I write about? My childhood was less than perfect—to be honest, it was quite dysfunctional. But who wants to hear about all that? I needed to write about something happy. *What are my happiest memories?*

I started to write about the backyard at the house I grew up in. I don't know what inspired me to write about that, but as I wrote more, the story unfolded more easily. It was a story about my sister.

Finally, I had completed it. I fired it off, after a quick spell check, and went on to another writing project. The only thing in my mind at that point was whether or not the woman compiling the anthology, Helen Polaski, would accept it or not.

A short time later that day, I was surprised when I saw an email in my mailbox from her. I quickly opened it to discover this reply. "Gwen—We like it—a lot. With a couple of minor additions, we feel this story would fit very well in our anthology. To personalize the story, can we have the name of your sister? And we would love to see you expand on each section a bit more. The story has a lot of porch qualities, but it lacks what we call teary eyes factor. We are searching for the heart in your throat feeling."

I was thrilled that they were even considering it! I stopped everything I was doing and pulled up my story, "Yard of My Dreams." As I reread it, I wondered what I was trying to say—that I loved the yard? Or was I telling the story of my love for my sister?

My heart started to pound as I pecked at the keyboard. The story of my childhood—my memories of the times I shared with my sister—flowed through my fingertips and onto the screen. I didn't stop. I wrote and wrote until the very last word appeared on the screen in front of me: "Remember this—the greatest treasures in life are just outside your back door."

Tears rolled down my face. How I missed my sister. Why hadn't I remembered those wonderful times we had together—the bond we shared that ran so deep? What had happened to that?

My sister and I were not speaking to each other at the time I sat there in front of the computer screen. After a horrible argument the month before, we had agreed we needed to just stay out of each other's lives. We were just too different—incompatible. So, we hadn't spoken or emailed or anything for over a month. I didn't realize how much I missed her until the moment I sent her a copy of the story—that very day.

I didn't care if she answered me. I just needed her to know that, no matter what, I loved her. I wanted her to know that, even though we aren't on the same wavelength sometimes, she is still my best friend.

I sent the story to Helen at *Forget Me Knots...from the Front Porch.* Then I sat back and cried, my shoulders shaking and tears pouring down my face; I just sat there staring at the screen. It didn't take too long, and I heard back from Helen.

"Gwen—I love it! We're proud to have your story included in *Forget Me Knots...from the Front Porch,*" she wrote.

I was excited, but there was something else I felt. The fact that my story was going to be published in a book was thrilling, but I felt this overwhelming calm and peace wash over me. Just then I noticed I had another email—from my sister!

I was almost afraid to open it—since the last time we spoke, we were so hurtful to each other.

"Gwen, it is a wonderful story. You write so well. I am sorry that I was so hurtful to you. I wish I could be the person you see me as in your story. I love you," Michelle wrote in her email.

My eyes filled with tears of joy—I had my sister back. I know it will take forgiveness on both our parts, but there is hope. I missed her so much, that at times I thought my heart was breaking.

I quickly emailed Helen Polaski without a second thought. I needed to tell her of the amazing things that came out of her encouraging press on me to talk with my heart—to tell my story from deep within. I felt I needed to thank her for that.

Helen wrote back to me right away, "Gwen and Michelle—thank you. Thank you for letting me be a part of your life today. If God worked through me for this reunion, I feel very much blessed indeed. Now I'm crying."

I chatted with Helen for a little while, telling her how my heart was filled with such joy at being able to reach out to my sister in forgiveness and in love. God placed his hand on my shoulder that day—He helped me find a way to reach out to my sister through my writing. He is amazing! I know that we are prompted so much—nudged by God—and we don't even recognize His gentle touch. I am so glad that my senses were aware that day. I am glad I listened to His nudge.

Footprints on the Folders

By Bonnie Compton Hanson
Santa Ana, California, United States

"It's past 10:00 p.m., dear," my husband called, "and you're already worn out. How long do you plan to stay up?"

I glanced at my watch.

"I don't know. Chat might still come. I'd hate for the house to be dark when he got here."

"He has a key. Besides, he's always here by 8:30 p.m. when he's coming. Your computer can use a day off in this hot weather, and so can you. He'll be here tomorrow night. Meanwhile, you better get some rest."

Yawning, I nodded, then turned off the light in my study. My PC had suddenly crashed that morning. Since I had a project deadline the following week, I had called my computer expert son at work for advice. When Chat heard the symptoms, he sighed. "No, Mom, you won't be able to fix that problem by yourself. If I get out early from my class tonight, I'll come down to check things out. Otherwise, I'll be there tomorrow night for sure."

I felt as bad about calling on him for help as I felt about my PC being down. Both Chat and his new bride, Jeanne, worked long hours, with mind-numbing commutes. Plus both went to school at night and were involved in a full calendar of church activities. It wasn't fair to ask him to drive that extra hour each way to our house in the next county—especially in this blistering heat wave. But I didn't know where else to turn with that deadline over my head.

Unfortunately, this wasn't my first such emergency. That's why Chat always kept a set of keys to our house.

All day long I had worked with portable file boxes in the screened-in "garden room" at the back of our house, arranging and rearranging the folders in them to do that project. I had kept the door wide open as I worked, trying to keep cool. The file boxes were now neatly arranged around the garden room floor. So if he could just get my computer up and running again—

Humming "All Through the Night," I went around the house turning off lights, covering the bird cage, closing and locking the front door and kitchen door. Back in the garden room to close and lock that door, I glanced at the file boxes again. Immediately, I started thinking about that project. Maybe I could get just a bit more done before I turned out the light! So I set to work feverishly, until—

"Bonnie!" Don called. "I thought you were going to bed!"

"Be right there!" I quickly re-straightened the file boxes, shut and locked the garden room door, flicked out the lights, and hurried to our bedroom. As I got into bed, I prayed, "Dear God, please have Chat just go on home from school tonight and get some rest. Thank You for taking care of him. And for taking care of us, too." I fell asleep the minute my head hit the pillow.

Next thing I knew, a bright light woke me up—that and a few muffled sounds. I glanced at the clock. Two-thirty in the morning: Chat must have come after all! Jumping out of bed, I called, "Chat!"

Suddenly, I heard bumping sounds. That must be him! Throwing on my robe, I ran barefoot to my study, where he'd be working on my computer. "Chat, is that you?"

But it was dark. No one was there. More bumping sounds. Where were they coming from? And where had that bright light come from I saw earlier?

I flicked on the hall light and ran to the living room. "Chat!" I called again. "Don't leave yet! Let me fix you something to eat before you go."

But the living room was also empty, and the front door and kitchen doors still securely locked. Oh, that's right—he probably used the garden room door so he wouldn't disturb us! Why, he must've finished working on my PC just about the time I woke up, then turned off the lights, and was now leaving the same way.

Rushing to the dark garden room, I noticed the door was wide open. He must have been in such a rush he forgot to close and lock it.

"Chat! Chat!" I called, hurrying outside. "Don't go yet, Honey. Wait up!" Why, he'd forgotten to close the door!

But nobody was there. Not outside on the sidewalk either. Nothing but twinkling stars, some scurrying bugs, and startled cats.

Maybe he was already out front getting into his car! But when I ran to the front door and flung it open, there was nothing there, either, except for a chirping cricket.

But those lights, those sounds—I know they were real! *Dear God, had I really just imagined it all?*

My heart racing, I returned to bed to toss and turn all the rest of the night. First thing the next morning, I called Chat. "Honey, were you here last night?"

"No, Mom, my class got out too late. But I'll be there tonight for sure." Feeling relieved, but rather foolish, I went back to the garden room to continue my project in the daylight. Surprise! Half the file boxes had been knocked over, and there were folders and papers everywhere! What in the world had happened? Even though I had run through that room in a mad rush during the night, I didn't remember touching any of the boxes.

Then I saw footprints—heavy, black footprints from a large man's boots—all over those folders. I had been barefoot the night before. Chat had not come. And my husband had slept through it all. So those footprints belonged to someone else—someone who had managed to break in through that garden room door. Someone wearing muddy boots. The "bright light" that woke me up may have been a flashlight slipping past my bedroom. The bumping sounds: my file boxes falling over. Normally, I might have slept through it all. Especially since I was so tired. But last night, God helped me wake up just in time. My calling out "Chat!" must have panicked the would-be robber. Whirling about, he made a mad dash back toward the garden room door, knocking the file boxes over, spilling out the folders, then stepping on them with heavy, muddy boots.

I'm thankful that my intruder didn't have a gun, or at least didn't use one. I'm thankful that Chat did come the next night. My PC is now just fine, thank you. And, yes, I finished my project in time. But mostly, every time I happen to pull out a file folder that has a heavy, black footprint on the cover, I'm thankful that God does watch over us every minute of every day. And all night long, as well!

"He who watches over you will...neither slumber nor sleep...The Lord will keep you from all harm."   Psalm 121:3,5

Rekindling a Friendship

By P. Jeanne Davis
Philadelphia, Pennsylvania, United States

I have no childhood memories of visiting any relatives on my father's side, though we lived within a few miles of one another in Philadelphia. I didn't know at the time that this was because of ongoing hostilities between my grandfather and his daughter, Jane. Over the years, I've learned that my father avoided socializing with most of his family because of the situation.

There was one cousin, however, who did come with Uncle Bill and Aunt Marie to play. Her name was Shirley. Our fathers were brothers and kept close throughout this time. Shirley and I were both only children, and she was a few years older than me, but this didn't seem to matter.

But eventually my parents moved out of the area to a farm, and sadly, Shirley came no more. I now had a big grassy yard, but not my playmate, and I thought of her often.

When I was 18 years old, I moved back to my hometown to attend college. A lot had changed by then. My grandfather was deceased, and my father, at 46, was in poor health. The only time I saw all my father's family was at his funeral that year. But Shirley and her mother were not there. My Uncle Bill had died, and his wife, Marie, had remarried. She and Shirley had moved to another state.

I tried to imagine Shirley then at 21. Was she married? Did she have children?

I stayed in Philadelphia, where I eventually married and raised two sons. Often, my thoughts would reflect on my childhood memories with Shirley.

Many years later, the desire to connect with my father's family re-emerged when we received an invitation to a family reunion in England from my husband's side of the family. I knew my grandfather had emigrated from England, as well, so I mentioned to my husband, John, how great it would be to get my family together here.

But it was Shirley, in particular, that I wanted to find. *How many of my relatives would be living?* I wondered.

I recalled a second cousin who had a business and was amazed when I found him in the directory. Francis was nearly 80 years old and still in real estate.

"You're Tom's daughter," he said. "Your father and I were buddies as boys. I'll have to tell my brother, Ralph, you called."

Francis went on to share some of his memories of my father with me, but he didn't have the key information I was looking for.

"I can't tell you anything about your Uncle Bill's daughter. You need to call your Aunt Jane. She knows where she is living. I'll find her number."

"Let's get together," I said. *This was a good starting point*, I thought.

Francis gave me the names and addresses of most of my father's siblings and cousins who were now quite elderly. They all were very enthusiastic about a get-together.

I reached Aunt Jane, now 90 years old, at her nursing home. "You're my brother, Tom's, daughter. I want to meet you. I will come to the reunion." She had kept in touch with Shirley all these years and would tell her about our upcoming get-together and that she talked with me.

Before the week was over, I was listening to Shirley's emotion-filled voice on the telephone. "You remember me! My dad was your uncle. I can remember playing with you, Patsy, in your alley. We have gotten separated through the years, and I'm glad to hear from you."

The feeling in her voice sang like a song. "I will try to come to the reunion with my family," she promised.

All this time, her only contact with the family had been our aunt. But when she asked Aunt Jane about me, she could get no information.

I met my Aunt Jane for the first time at this first gathering that my quest to find Shirley had sparked. Until now, she had only been a name to me. I also got acquainted with many distant cousins, as well. In an emotionally driven moment, my Aunt Jane took my hand as she was leaving and with tears whispered, "You and your husband have reunited our family after all these years." Yet, there remained much sadness in her face when discussing the estrangement with my grandfather and their inability to be reconciled.

It was wonderful meeting so many of my long lost cousins, but one face I searched for in vain.

To my disappointment, Shirley hadn't come to the family festivities. *What had happened?*

During the following week, I called Shirley. "I was going to get in touch with you also, Patsy. Can we meet at my home soon?" she asked excitedly. Apparently, she was unable to acquire transportation to the event.

We did get together, and the day we spent together was just the beginning of many such visits over the next two years. It was a day of sharing distant memories and photographs and trying to catch up on the many years since our childhood in the city.

Sadly, a few weeks after our meeting, Aunt Jane died. I know our aunt felt much pleasure in knowing she had brought two cousins together at last.

Since our reunion, Shirley and I have kept in contact and rekindled our friendship. Shirley filled me in on that portion of my childhood lost to me through my family's estrangement. We have become like sisters to each other. We share a strong family resemblance, even as our fathers looked much alike. Many of our life experiences and interests have been similar.

Shirley and I both lost our dads while still adolescents, were both stay-at-home moms, and both raised sons. Close church ties and worship are an integral part of both our families' lives.

We are so thankful to have found each other. We know God has brought us together in His own way after 40 years.

I Almost Threw It All Away

By Shirley Jump
Fort Wayne, Indiana, United States

When I first started writing, I was young and sure any success came from my own abilities, not some power on high. But as I got older, I began to seek God more in my life and to understand that every success was a gift from Him. With that, came the realization that I wanted more of my life to be directed toward God, too. I just wasn't sure how to do that or whether my writing even figured into the equation.

In the years while I wrote, polished, revised, sent...and got rejected, there were many times when I questioned whether I was on the right path. However, as frustrating as those years were and as hard as it was to write all those books just to see them get shot down, they were a learning lesson from God—it just took me quitting to see the lesson in all its strength.

I truly believe God doesn't hand you anything you aren't ready for. If I had sold my first book (or any of the other early ones), I wouldn't have been ready for a career. I sure *thought* I was ready, but in all honesty, I wasn't. I hadn't been tested yet and, thus, hadn't built the fortitude I needed for the difficult path ahead.

I hit a crisis in my writing career in the summer of 2001. I received a rejection that was simply the latest in a towering pile of letters turning my work away. I was frustrated and angry, and I threw out everything in my office. I wiped out my hard drive, tossed out the dusty unpublished manuscripts, and then sat down and cried.

My husband encouraged me to put it all back, which I did. But I didn't write. I sat down and prayed instead, telling God I wasn't sure anymore if this was the direction I should take. Maybe I was meant to write something else. Or maybe I wasn't meant to write at all. I asked God to please send me a sign, something to keep my hope going and show me the path I should travel.

A few days later, an encouraging letter came in the mail from an editor who had read my latest romance manuscript. She wanted to buy it, if I made a few changes. Two weeks later, I had signed with a new agent who believed in me and was ready to take my career to the next level. I sold that book in December and embarked on a new chapter in my writing.

However, I wasn't quite happy yet. I'd had the sign I'd been looking for, but I wanted to be sure I was traveling in the right direction. I searched my heart and soul looking at why I had chosen to write romantic comedies, of all the kinds of books I could write. For a long time, I had said I wanted to write romance, without ever quantifying why. I asked God if this was where my talent should be directed. After all, I loved to read books by Stephen King and John Grisham—maybe I should be writing horror or suspense?

The answer came to me in a whisper, a message that went straight to my heart.

Romantic comedies are stories that celebrate love, family, commitment, and laughter. In a world increasingly fraught with violence, terrorism, and unhappy endings, writing books that reaffirm people's belief in love seems the right thing to do. I'm not a high-drama suspense writer. I'm not a horror writer. I'm definitely not a poetry writer, though I've tried my hand at all of those forms. Until I hit my stride in romantic comedy, I always felt slightly off kilter—like I was trying to fit a square peg into a triangular hole. I had three sides right, but I needed

to learn how to shave off that fourth side—the one that symbol-
ized all my misconceptions—and listen to God's direction

That message was solidified when I went to the women's
retreat at my church. The speaker, Martha Fellure, talked about
how each of us has a purpose in God's eyes. We're not just here
to take up space and air, but to truly serve Him and each other in
a way only we can do. God wants us to use our individual talents to serve that purpose and to spread His messages.

I sat in the audience and felt as if Martha were speaking
directly to me, emphasizing the message I'd heard in my heart
days before. I had chosen a path that made me feel right with
my God.

I am writing stories that reinforce His messages about
commitment and love. And I go to sleep each night, proud of
the work I have done and anxious to get back to it the next day.

My sign from God was so quiet that I might have missed
it, had I been looking in another direction. But I took the time to
get still—with myself and with my thoughts—and when I did,
God talked to me. No matter where this career takes me finan-
cially, I know in my heart that I have chosen a path that brings
me internal satisfaction and a personal feeling of success that is
derived from serving God and making Him a part of every word
I compose.

8

Of Love and Marriage

The Lord God said, "It is not good for the man to be alone.
I will make a helper suitable for him." ... For this reason
a man will leave his father and mother and be united
to his wife, and they will become one flesh.
— Genesis 2:18, 24

God Gave Me A Prince

By Jennifer Anne F. Messing
Portland, Oregon, United States

"Do you need a ride home, Jennifer?" asked the young American gentleman I'd just met. His warm brown eyes looked at me intently.

"Actually, my parents' driver is coming to pick me up," I answered. "But thanks anyway, Michael."

"Can I walk you to the lobby and wait with you 'til your driver arrives?" Michael was a man who was not going to let go of me easily. I sensed this at once.

"Of course," I replied, smiling at him. He appeared to be a genuine, tenderhearted fellow. We had both just attended the wedding rehearsal of mutual friends, Andy and Jaylyn, on that sunny afternoon in April 1989. They were to be married the next day in a garden wedding at the gorgeous Century Park Sheraton of Manila, Philippines.

Jaylyn and I were young, single, working Filipina women. Our families had known each other for several years. Andy and Michael had come to the Philippines on short-term missions trips every year for four consecutive years. This year their team came to Manila not only to minister, but also to attend the marriage celebration of Andy and Jaylyn. Now here I was, honored to be asked by Jaylyn to be a bridesmaid. Michael was a groomsman. Michael and I had fun chatting for over 20 minutes until my driver arrived. *Why am I excited that I will see him again tomorrow at the wedding?* I thought.

The following day Mom and I both had our hair done at a salon. My parents were good friends of Jaylyn's parents, and they had been asked to participate in an important part of the wedding ceremony. We were all dressed and ready to go at 4:00 p.m. When I entered our living room wearing a peach-colored bridesmaid's gown, my Dad whistled.

"Wow!" he exclaimed. "You look beautiful. Are you the bride?"

I laughed good-naturedly, thinking to myself, *I wish I were a bride today!* I smiled at Dad, and replied, "No, but I've heard that after a second stint as a bridesmaid, you get promoted."

"I've never heard that before," Mom interjected. We all chuckled, got into the car, and left. The wedding proceeded as planned, and all went beautifully.

But as I stood watching Jaylyn and Andy exchange wedding vows, my eyes filled with tears. While I rejoiced with them for the new life they were beginning together, the tears I shed at that moment were tears of sadness.

Wasn't this the way life should have turned out for me, too? Meet a devoted, loving Christian man while in my 20's, fall in love, get married, then live happily ever after? That's what I had hoped for, what my mom had prayed for, wasn't it? Yet here I was, a 23-year-old single mom. My precious one-year-old daughter, Celine, was at home with her nanny.

I had met Celine's father, Alvin*, when I was 20, and we were both students at a six-month live-in discipleship training school. Students there could not date or go steady with a fellow student for the six-month duration of the school.

Attracted to each other, Alvin and I had disobeyed this rule from the start. The school's aim was to help one get to know God intimately and become discipled through Bible study, mentoring, and prayer support. Obviously, Alvin and I were both immature in our walk with God.

Our leaders assured us that God loved us and that they did, too, but at the same time, said we needed to discontinue our relationship. We never listened to them, and because we always saw each other in secret, soon our relationship also became intimate.

We finished school and, shortly afterward, eloped. I married Alvin against my school leaders'—and most importantly, against my family's—wishes. My mom and two older brothers had seen in Alvin what I was too naive to see: immaturity, someone who was ill-prepared for the responsibilities of married life, even partying and drugs.

On our wedding night, Alvin had a bitter argument with one of his female cousins who lived nearby. Their quarrel became so severe, and Alvin got so enraged and out of control, that he punched two of his female cousins. And all this on my wedding night! A dark sense of foreboding came over me. *What have I gotten into?* I wondered.

Little did I know, it was only the beginning.

Only two months into our marriage, our own severe quarrels began. I discovered that Alvin was jealous and suspicious. He watched my every move closely. Since he knew my family disapproved of our marriage, he didn't want me to call or get in touch with them, which hurt me deeply.

Alvin didn't have a job and didn't appear to be trying very hard to get one. Sometimes he would take off with his friends for several days, and I never really knew where he went.

After six months, I became pregnant. When my mom found out I was pregnant, though she had opposed our marriage, she invited us to live in a spare bedroom in my family's home for as long as we needed. My mom was concerned about my health and the baby's health, plus she knew Alvin still did not have a job. My mom also encouraged Alvin to finish college at night and paid for his tuition.

As my pregnancy progressed, our explosive fights escalated. Finally, two weeks before my due date, Alvin left and never returned. Two weeks later, with my parents' loving support, I gave birth to my first child, a beautiful baby girl I named Celine Marie.

I never saw Alvin again, and Alvin never saw Celine. Several weeks later, I found out from Alvin's friends that he had never gone to college at night as we supposed. He had partied and even had affairs with different women.

Crushed and heartbroken, I don't even know how I made it through those early months of caring for Celine. Fortunately, my family gathered around me to offer their love and support.

During the next few weeks, I recommitted my life to Jesus. I repented of my sins, my rebellion against my parents, and of the immoral relationship with Alvin prior to marriage.

Though difficult to do at age 22, I told my parents I would live in their home once again in submission to their authority. I also told them I would not remarry without their blessing.

I began to attend church regularly with my parents and Celine. I also became a member of a ladies' Bible study group.

God began doing wonderful new things in my life. I landed a job as an executive secretary at the Manila office of a French perfume company. While I was at work, Celine stayed home with a full-time nanny.

By the time Celine was seven months old, a few eligible men, at different times, had asked me out on dates. I accepted a few invitations, but very cautiously. I kept praying, "Lord, please show me who You want for me this time around. I want Your will for my life." And I sincerely wanted God's will—whether it meant being reconciled to Alvin, being single forever, or getting married again.

As I prayed and sought God, however, it became clear to me that God called me to a brand new start in life, not a reconciliation. My pastor's and parents' advice also confirmed this.

So I kept up with my new job, developed Christian friendships, and took care of Celine at night after work. A friend from my church gave me the name of a lawyer through whom, she advised, I might obtain a legal annulment. After receiving much wise counsel from my parents, I filed for a legal annulment.

One evening, I received a phone call from an old friend, Jaylyn. She said she was to be wed the following month to Andy Trogen, a Christian man from Portland, Oregon. "Would you be a bridesmaid at my wedding, Jennifer?" she asked.

"Sure," I replied, feeling honored. "I would love to!"

****

Now I stood there, teary-eyed, watching as Andy and Jaylyn exchanged wedding vows. I prayed that someday I would find a Christian man who would love me and want to spend the rest of his life with me and also be a father to Celine.

Later, during the reception, Michael came and spoke with me. I enjoyed his kindheartedness and his intelligence. Actually, he monopolized most of my time at the reception. He told me he was going with the mission team to different cities in the Philippines for the next several days. Would I be free to join him for dinner when he got back to Manila, before he returned to Portland? I told him that would probably be fine. I asked him to call me when he got back to Manila. Then I took a picture of Celine out of my purse.

"This is my one-year-old daughter, Celine," I said hesitantly. I wanted any man seriously interested in pursuing me to know about her at once. Michael looked at the picture, then smiled.

"She sure is cute! She must be a joy to have around." Then he paused, and added, "Jaylyn told me you have a daughter, Jennifer. But I'm glad you did, too. When I get back to

Portland, I'm going to keep on praying for you and Celine every day."

Later, after we had talked, I noticed that Michael approached my parents and introduced himself.

Before Michael returned to Portland, we saw each other again. Jaylyn and Andy did not leave to go on their honeymoon immediately, so they invited all the groomsmen and bridesmaids for an evening out at Café Adriatico.

Café Adriatico's Spanish-style architecture and elegant, quaint interior never seemed more picturesque than on that night. I had a delightful time. I sat beside Michael, and we laughed and talked and got better acquainted. His deep-set brown eyes gazed into mine so intensely. . .almost as though they were asking without words, "Who are you, Jennifer? You are a mystery to me. I want to get to know you better. I want to know who you really are deep down inside."

During the months after Michael returned to Portland, I often thought of him, especially while I read my Bible at night. I started to pray more earnestly. *Did God have something in store for Michael and me?*

My pastor encouraged everyone to maintain total purity before marriage, and he also exhorted us to truly seek God's guidance about who God wanted us to marry.

"I believe Michael is the man God wants me to marry," I told my parents one evening. "I've been praying, and that's what God is saying."

Since Michael had been gone a few months and I had not received any letters or phone calls from him, my mom replied, "We better pray harder then."

I continued to pray about it, as did my parents.

My questions and prayers were answered when, two months later, my father received a letter from Michael. He reintroduced himself and basically informed my father of his intent to begin corresponding with me. My Dad voiced no objections.

I laughed with joy when Dad and Mom told me about Michael's letter.

"See, Mom," I said, "I told you—I think God is saying, 'It's Michael!'"

Not long after, I received a letter from Michael. Several weeks after that, he called long-distance. It was December 16th, my 24th birthday. During this phone call, we talked heart to heart. He told me he had been praying for Celine and me almost every day since leaving Manila. He also told me he wanted to come visit me for three weeks with the intent of pursuing marriage.

As Michael shared this, a growing peace enveloped my heart. I knew that God was moving in my life, bringing His will to pass. Before we ended our phone call, we decided he should come to Manila seven weeks later, in February 1990.

My parents were excited, and they told my brothers and my sister all about Michael. They also told our relatives, our pastor, and other close Christian friends. Everywhere I turned, I found favor and approval. How different it was from my first marriage! *So this is what it's like to pursue marriage with God's blessing,* I thought to myself.

Things began to happen quickly after Michael's phone call. The legal annulment of my first marriage was granted, and I was given time off from work during the weeks of Michael's visit. The day Michael arrived, and the moment we met again, my heart pounded. I gave him a warm hug, and we sat and visited in my home that evening. He also met Celine for the first time, and she welcomed Michael into her life quite easily.

During the next three weeks, I experienced the most glorious courtship and romance of my life! Michael and I spent each day together. Celine and her nanny were often with us on our dates. We visited my friends and relatives, took Celine shopping, went sightseeing, went to the beach, and went out for candlelight dinners. Of course, we went to Café Adriatico once again. This time we chose a table for two in a dimly lit corner. We gazed into each other's eyes, and held hands.

"I love you, Jennifer," Michael said. "I don't want to live my life without you. Will you marry me?"

"Yes," I replied, filled with awe and wonder. "Yes, I will marry you." With joy, I received the engagement ring he placed on my finger. On October 20 of that year, I married Michael Robert Messing—the most wonderful Christian man I've ever met—with my parents' blessings. With God's strength, we had followed a path of purity—and our first kiss was our wedding kiss.

We have lived in Portland, Oregon, since, and we now have three children. Our 11 years of marriage have been filled with love, passion, and adventure. No marriage is problem-free, but our faith in God continues to help us overcome obstacles. Whenever I reflect on what God has done in my life, I thank Him for giving me a prince.

Three Nudges and A Shove

By Kristin Dreyer Kramer
Andover, Massachusetts, United States

I've never handled nudges well. Actually, if someone nudges me the slightest bit, I'm the type to respond with a shove.

It's been said that my tendency to keep my feet firmly planted wherever I decide they belong comes from my Dutch blood. Apparently, the Dutch are all as stubborn as I am. Considering the other Dutch people I know, it could very well be true—though it frightens me to think of an entire country of people just like my family and me.

Whatever the reason, though, I've never been one to follow advice—especially if it's unsolicited advice. I prefer to do things *my way*—no matter how poorly my way works.

Once, however, I followed a nudge. Now, I didn't follow it right away, mind you. It took a few nudges and a shove, actually. But eventually I listened—and I still can't believe where it led.

The first gentle nudge came in February, a couple of years ago. At that point, everything seemed to have gone wrong. My dream job had turned into a nightmare, and I had just been thrown from my longest relationship in years—it had lasted six whole weeks. To make matters worse, it was February in Michigan, and I hadn't seen the sun in months.

That's when an old college friend showed up for a visit, and we spent some time getting caught up. When we moved from telling stories to saying goodbyes, my friend said the same thing he'd been saying for the last three years: "You know, you really need to come out and visit me sometime."

And I nodded and said the same thing *I'd* been saying for the last three years: "Yeah, May." *That's far enough away,* I assured myself. *He'll forget by then.*

But this time was different. This time he wasn't about to let me off that easily. So that's when I got the first little nudge.

"OK. When?"

I was stunned. I thought we had an agreement. He'd keep inviting me, and I'd keep pretending that I was actually going to visit someday. But I didn't really *want* to visit. He lived in Toronto. That was a six-hour drive away (in a different country, no less), and my old car could barely make it across town. But he had me in a corner. I *had* just agreed to visit, hadn't I?

"Well, um…"

I told him about the plans I'd already made. I was headed to Nebraska for a weekend. And then I was going to Colorado the beginning of April. "So maybe May," I told him. *Yeah, May. That was far enough away. He'd forget by then.*

But he didn't forget. It wasn't long before he called me and told me that he'd been invited to a friend's wedding on May 20th—and he wanted me to be his guest.

"You said you were coming in May, right?"

Another gentle nudge.

"Well…" What could I say? He had caught me. I couldn't tell him that I really didn't mean it, could I? "…OK."

But I still hadn't made my final decision. *Maybe,* I thought, *I can still get out of it.*

The week before my trip to Toronto, I finally found my loophole. I was out with some friends on Friday night, and my car died. There was something seriously wrong with it, and there was no way it was going to make the six-hour drive. I took my car's problems as a sign that I was right after all—I shouldn't go to Toronto. I was relieved—right up until the moment when my sister-in-law spoke up. "Why don't you just take the train?" she asked. "You wouldn't have to drive. You could just sit back and relax."

Suddenly, I was getting nudges from all directions.

But the third nudge finally worked. Of course, it wasn't because I was finally ready to give in. It was because I was in love with the idea of spending 10 hours on a quiet train with nothing to do but read and write. And I already had a couple of days off—I figured I might as well use them.

I hopped on the train that Friday and rode through the afternoon and into the night, across the state and into Canada—surrounded by gaggles of cackling women on exciting girls-only trips to the city to see *The Lion King,* doing very little reading or writing.

That night, my friend and I wandered through the city for a while before retiring to his apartment and telling more stories over a bag of all-dressed chips. Then we got up the next morning, split a pot of strong coffee, and headed back into the city for the wedding.

We were early, so we stood outside the church enjoying the warm spring day. As we did, we were joined by someone I'd remembered from my college English courses—Charlene. She greeted us and stepped into our little group, along with her cousin, Paul, who immediately caught my eye. He was a quiet, handsome guy with beautiful eyes and a smile that could light up a room (or so I told everyone who would listen for the next week), and I had every intention of getting to know him as much as I could.

And that's exactly what I did. The two of us ended up spending the evening chatting and dancing and making our way through those initial get-to-know-you questions. By the end of the night, neither one of us was quite ready to walk away—so we made plans to go out the next night.

Paul managed to get six passes for a popular club downtown. It wasn't exactly a place to chat, but it would have to do. Since the next day was a holiday, the club was open late—and I was ready to stay there as long as possible. So even though I had a train to catch at 6:00 a.m., I stayed out until 3:30 a.m.

When we finally decided to leave, our group made its way across the packed dance floor. And as we did, Paul reached out and took my hand. His fingers intertwined in mine. And though it took me by surprise, it felt natural—as though that was just the way it was supposed to be. I didn't want to let go.

I couldn't have slept on the way home if I'd tried. I was too giddy-happy-excited to rest. Instead, I just lounged in my tiny train seat and grinned groggily.

For a while, Paul and I kept in touch through pages-long emails. By the time I once again boarded the train for Toronto— just three weeks later—we had already planned Fourth of July weekend at my family's cottage and an August camping weekend followed by Paul's sister's wedding. Neither of us ever considered that we wouldn't last that long.

But there was a problem—a big, 400-mile problem. I had always joked that long-distance relationships were the only ones I could handle—because I didn't really have the time to deal with a real relationship. But at that point, I was pretty sure I was ready to deal with it. Unfortunately, that wasn't an option. And I wasn't sure how long I could keep taking days off and buying train tickets. I was afraid of what would happen.

Then, just over a month after Paul and I met, I lost my job. At the time, of course, I was crushed. Devastated. I thought my life was crumbling around me. Now I realize that it was just a nudge—more like a push, really. A shove. I had been praying for an answer, and I had found it. Sure, it wasn't *my* way, but suddenly it was *the* way.

So Paul and I were pretty much thrown into our new life together. I became a freelance writer—living off my savings and the occasional paying client—and a semi-permanent fixture at Paul's parents' house. I already knew that my future was pretty clear. I knew that wherever Paul and I were headed, we were headed there together.

Even though it took a few nudges, Paul and I ended up crossing paths—and in no time, our paths became one. The next February, Paul proposed, and we got married the following October.

So I guess that no matter how Dutch-stubborn I am—no matter how firmly I've planted my feet—it only takes a solid shove or two to get me headed in the right direction.

Lo, How a Rose E'er Blooming

By Rusty Fischer
Orlando, Florida, United States

I had no one to pick up at the airport that desolate Christmas Eve—not a single, solitary soul—but if I had to sit in my one-bedroom apartment and stare at my little Charlie Brown Christmas tree blink on and off for even one second more, I was going to actually do it—and I didn't want to. Not really. At least, I didn't think so…

So I got dressed, trying to imagine what I would wear if I did have someone to pick up, and I drove to the airport slowly, feeling the last silent flickers of hope dance around my lonely heart.

Perhaps I would run into a long-lost friend among the bustling holiday crowd. Maybe I'd take a seat next to another hopeful, lonely soul and strike up a holiday conversation about something inane, like the origins of mistletoe. Who knows?

When I finally got there, I put quarters into the meter by my parking space. I was literally buying time.

The airport was crowded, but I figured that was the point—more people, more opportunities for connection. Contact. Conversation.

It was nearly midnight on Christmas Eve, and holiday travelers were rushing to and fro, hurrying to catch their late-night flights so they could wake up—at home—on Christmas morning.

I was the only one there without a carry-on bag or a rolling piece of sleek, black luggage full of cheesy, last-minute gifts and Santa boxer shorts.

I worried, for an instant, that someone might find me out—discover that I wasn't really traveling anywhere—and that I was just hanging around in some pathetic, last-ditch attempt to be with other people in some naively meaningful manner, to carve out any kind of holiday for myself that I possibly could.

But the moment quickly passed. Who would give my presence there a second thought? No one looked at me. No one saw me. Not a single face turned in my direction or even gave me a quick once over. No one even smiled.

They were all wrapped up in their busy schedules, and even the people who were traveling together seemed flustered and mean. They rushed each other and scowled ungratefully as they argued over who would carry what bag and then walked single file down the long hallway. They nagged about forgotten coffee machines left on back home.

One young couple fought in the gift shop because he bought a shiny new paperback she said they couldn't afford.

I found a snack bar and bought a petrified hot dog, greasy fries, and a runny chocolate milkshake. I knew I should lose some weight, but this was a small Christmas treat to myself. And it tasted good. Besides, there was always the New Year.

If I was still around, that was...

I started to clean some mustard off of my sweater, but then stopped myself. Maybe when someone noticed it, they would actually pay attention to me—speak to me. It was all I wanted for Christmas. My only wish—my one, small holiday hope: To hear another human voice speaking in my direction.

I wandered the ticket counters and shoeshine stands for a while, waiting for someone to speak up—to look at me and smile—or even nod on their quick way by. But no one did.

Carols played cheerily over the Muzak high above me as businessmen in fine suits stepped on my toes. Mothers clinging to bulging shopping bags sighed loudly as a signal for me to move out of their way. An old woman pushed me aside with an elbow that was surprisingly strong. Two punks pointed at my sweater and laughed. A pretty stewardess in a tight uniform rolled her eyes when she caught me looking at her.

A knot formed in my stomach and fear clawed at my chest as I wondered if I was invisible. I found a crowded Delta gate and took a vacant seat across from the window. Blinking lights strung around the ticket counter winked on and off in a forced ode to holiday cheer.

An old woman across from me dabbed at her nose with a tissue. Her stockings sagged, and her shoes looked scuffed and tired. She clutched a large purse to her chest and stared off into space. I imagined a story about her in my mind, one full of heartbreak and woe, of spoiled children who never called and grandchildren who wouldn't recognize her if they passed her on the street.

I rose to approach her, to save her—and perhaps myself—when a large, happy family, booming with the announcement that they'd found some cold medicine, swallowed her into their midst. Her smile made the Christmas lights seem dim.

I should have known better. I *was* the only one without a friend, a wife, a lover, a family. I'd known it all along. I picked at the crusty glob of mustard on my sweater and imagined the many ways I might end my life. I was a gentle man, so a blade or gun wouldn't do. I lived in a cheap apartment, so I couldn't run a hose from my exhaust pipe to the front seat. But I did have a gas oven.

I was already imagining the outfit I'd wear for my final hour when I rose to leave the airport. But just then, the sound of crinkling plastic poked into my morbid thoughts, and I looked to find its source. A single red rose surrounded with baby's breath and wrapped in dime store plastic crackled nearby in a pale, young hand.

I stopped and watched as a young man, more boy than man really, quietly walked into the crowd at the gate. He looked fresh and scrubbed, his hair wet and slicked back. His large hands fumbled with his stiff shirt collar and smoothed the crinkled plastic wrap around his thin, frail flower.

The boy had a pale complexion, and rosy apples stood out in his pale cheeks, and although he wasn't smiling, I knew he would be soon when whoever the rose was for—a girlfriend, perhaps, or even a fiancé—stepped off of the plane and into his waiting arms.

I stopped and turned back to the window as the whine of a jet engine loomed in the distance. A plane was pulling up to the gate. I hesitated for a moment and then walked over to join the crowd at the window. I said nothing, merely regarded the boy's stiff hair gel, the label on his imitation dress shirt, and the scuffed heels of his bargain dress shoes.

All around the boy, people jostled and shoved, complained, and accused as they tried to get a better look out the window. But the boy didn't wince or ball up his fist, or spit or shout or curse. He only moved aside and let others in front of him, a wan smile rising to his innocent face.

I forgot about my gas oven and stood back to await the arrival of the plane as if I, too, had someone to greet—as if I, too, had high hopes for a friend or a lover's arrival.

None of us noticed that the clock above our heads had just struck midnight.

I watched as families departed the plane. Loved ones rushed into each other's arms for quick hugs before disappearing down the terminal to collect their baggage and hurry home. A hundred "Hello's" and "Merry Christmas's" were cried out and answered before the terminal was empty and there was only the boy and myself waiting for his mystery guest.

I waited in eager anticipation, as if I knew the girl myself. I hung back behind the ticket counter so the boy didn't think I was stalking him and smiled when a young girl finally stepped off of the plane. She was no beauty, but the smile on her frail face when she saw the boy waiting for her turned her into one immediately. He gave her the flower, so coveted, so carefully, and she took it gently as they hugged for a quick, but intense, moment. She looked at it often as they disappeared down the terminal, holding hands and whispering quietly as they planned a romantic holiday together.

Many things have happened in my life since that fateful night when a young pair of innocent strangers saved my life in a way that can only be called a true "nudge from God." Who else could have sent me to that airport? At just the right time? On just the right night? His night? Who else could have put that loving couple, that precious symbol of hope, those darling rays of light, directly in my path?

Right when I needed to see them the most...

Now, no matter how hectic or wild things get in my holiday season, I never forget to buy a single red rose on Christmas Eve.

It is one of my beautiful wife's favorite holiday traditions.

When Love Calls

By Violet Coetzee
Doringkloof, Centurion, Republic of South Africa

In the 1950's in rural South Africa, our children had to attend boarding schools from an early age because of the vast distances between farms and villages. Two of our three children, then aged 7 and 10 years old, were boarders at a small farm school about 70 miles from our farm. All the children in our area would be collected by the various parents in turn early on a Monday morning and taken to boarding school, and then be fetched again on Friday afternoon after school to go home for the weekend.

We produced various crops on the farm, but our main income was derived from buying sheep and cattle, which we then fattened for the large meat markets in the mining areas of Johannesburg. So it came to pass one week that my husband was away from the farm on business in Johannesburg. He stayed with his sister and her family for the few days that it would take to conclude his business, and I was alone on the farm with a few farm hands.

Around 12:00 one night, I was woken up by the insistent ringing of our telephone. I stumbled out of bed with my heart in my throat, as a telephone ringing at that time of night could only mean bad news. And so it was. My little seven-year-old son was very ill, and the matron at the boarding school was at her wits end. In those days, it was not so easy to get hold of a doctor when you were miles from anywhere, and the hostel was at least an hour's drive from the nearest village. My son had croup and was getting worse all the time, struggling for every breath. They wanted us to fetch him as soon as possible.

My heart sank. What was I going to do? My husband was at least six hours away, and the only vehicles left on the farm were our big truck, which I could not drive, and the tractors. I explained the situation to the matron and then told her how to ease my son's breathing by steaming him with eucalyptus leaves and Vicks Vaporub in a pot of boiling water. I would phone again in a while to hear if he was breathing any easier. As soon as it was light, I would send a farmhand with a message to my nearest neighbors (as they did not have a telephone) asking them to drive me to the school to fetch my son and take him to the doctor.

During the next few hours, I must have telephoned the matron a hundred times! Luckily, the first aid seemed to help, as he eventually began to breathe a little easier and fell asleep. The matron promised to stay with him in the dormitory for the rest of the night and to let me know if he again got worse.

I stoked the coal fire in the kitchen, bathed, and got dressed, as I knew that any further sleep was out of the question. Then I sat at the kitchen table shivering and drinking cup after cup of coffee, praying the long night over. Every so often, I would look out of the window at the white moonlit veldt, hoping for the first glimmer of dawn. Never had a winter's night been so long.

Around 6:00 a.m., still quite some time before daybreak, the dogs started barking, and I thought I heard the faint sound of a car approaching on the dirt road. I looked out and saw headlights dipping in and out of the trees that lined the farm road. I wondered who on earth it could possibly be at that time of the morning, but at the same time, I felt faintly relieved, because whoever it was could probably take me to fetch my son.

And then my mouth dropped open in astonishment. It was my husband who was not due home for another two days! I ran outside as he pulled into the driveway. He jumped out of the car and enfolded me in his strong arms, asking me what was wrong and why I had called him home. By this time, I was crying with relief and joy at seeing him. I blurted out my relief and worry, and we both got back into the car.

Only as we were driving away from the farm did I register what he had said when he first held me. He had asked why I had called him. On the way to the school, we pieced together both sides of our story.

He told me that he woke up just after 12:00 midnight with an overwhelming feeling that I needed him. He got out of bed, got dressed, woke his sister and her husband, and told them that I was calling him and that he was going home. They thought that he was crazy and told him to at least wait until the morning, but he would hear nothing of it. He drove as fast as he could, stopping only once to wake a sleepy petrol attendant to fill up his car. Exactly six hours later, he was on the farm.

We fetched our son just as the sun broke over the crisp clear veldt. The steaming eucalyptus and Vaporub had seen him through the night. After a thorough checkup, the doctor sent him home with more medicine and strict instructions for his treatment.

My sister-in-law telephoned later that day and was astonished to hear that her brother had been absolutely right in coming home in the middle of the night. She confirmed that they tried to talk him out of it when he had woken them up to say goodbye and that he had insisted that I was calling him. My heart had called him so intensely that he could not fail to heed its voice.

Sadly, we lost our wonderful son when he was just 32 years old, but that same love carried us and our two daughters through it all.

I am 85 years old this year, and I have been a widow for nearly seven years—years that I could never have imagined that I could have survived without my husband.

I believe that, by the Grace of God, the memory and reality of our love will remain with me until we meet again.

About the Author
who compiled this book

Vanessa K. Mullins

Vanessa K. Mullins is, first and foremost, a wife and mother. She and her family currently reside in Michigan.

Vanessa first started writing in her teenage years when she filled notebooks and notebooks with the poetry of a teenager in angst. Soon after college, marriage and family took first priority in her life. It wasn't until years later that she realized that, yes, in fact, she could have all of those things and her writing, too.

She and a close friend decided they would write novels. They started their own writing group and invited several friends. Six months later, Vanessa had finished her first full-length novel and had several articles published on the Internet. Vanessa has also completed a second novel—this time a young adult mystery—which is the first in a planned series. She also has a few other books on her shelves waiting for her to get back to them.

After several of her short works were accepted and published in various anthologies, Vanessa knew that she had something to offer the world. She became inspired to follow the callings of her heart—the nudges she believes God has been giving her all along—and to pursue her writing. The result of those repeated nudgings is the book you now hold in your hands, *Nudges from God, An Anthology of Inspiration*.

Email her with your thoughts/comments about the book at: vkmullins@comcast.net.

About the Cover Artist

Melissa Jane Szymanski

Melissa Jane Szymanski received a Bachelor of Fine Arts Degree from Siena Heights College in Adrian, Michigan. Her major was drawing. Melissa's work has been exhibited in several art shows in Michigan, including Cranbrook Institute of Science in Bloomfield, Ella Sharp Museum in Jackson, Buckham Gallery in Flint, The Orion Center in Lake Orion, and Paint Creek Center for the Arts in Rochester.

With a great eye for detail, portraits and figures have always been her strong point. Diana, her framer, says, "When Melissa does a portrait, it almost breathes."

Melissa's recent works include children and pets portrayed as angels done in colored pencil. She currently resides in Metro Detroit with her husband, Sam Mau, and their two Australian Cattle dogs, Wally and Rodeo.

You can email Melissa at: forgetmeknotsanthology @yahoo.com.

Contributor's Bios

Jozette Aaron has been writing fiction since 2000. Her work has been published on various web sites across the net, and she has had two of her books published, using her pen name Georgie DeSilva. Jozette has also contributed to the anthology, *Forget Me Knots... from the Front Porch.* She lives in Ontario, Canada, where she works as a Registered Nurse. www.aarondesilva.com

Linda Adams has been published in *The Writer's Journal, Mocha Memoirs, The Potomac Review, The Toastmaster,* and the anthology, *Let Us Not Forget,* a tribute to American veterans. She is currently co-writing a women's action adventure thriller set during the Civil War. Website: http://www.hackman-adams.com

Del Sylver Bates is a freelance writer who resides in Vero Beach, Florida, with her husband, Jon. After raising her three children, she decided to trade her apron in for a pen to fulfill her desire to lead the lost to the Saving Grace of Jesus Christ. To enjoy many of her poems and daily devotionals, visit her at www.Handstoblessu.com.

Robert Baumgart was born and raised in Flint, Michigan. He attended Kearsley High School where he was inspired by some of Michigan's most talented instructors. He joined the Air Force in 2000 and currently resides in Warner Robins, Georgia.

Alaine Benard has been published in parenting magazines, newspapers, books, and websites. She is editor and publisher of StormWatch, the monthly edition of her column. Alaine is currently completing her third book, an anthology of positive stories about children with ADHD. She works with differently-abled children in an elementary school. www.dixiesky.com/ADHD_Soaring

Alberta "Berta" Beversdorf has been a story teller, poet, and essayist for 30 years, inspired by the birth of her first daughter. She has written tributes, music for school plays, and PTA newsletters. As a girl, she was told by her dad that she had ink flowing in her veins. She believed him!

Glenda Thornhill Bozeman is a freelance writer, the mother of two, and the grandmother of four. She is currently writing her first book about the life of a Christian woman trapped in a self-destructive relationship of alcohol and sexual abuse. Email: glendagbo@aol.com or call (256) 736-8547.

Louise Classon is a freelance writer based in Gaithersburg, Maryland, who writes inspirational and nostalgia articles for pleasure, and environmental articles for a living. She is involved in Catholic charismatic activities, such as prayer team ministry and prayer groups, and is the managing editor for *Shared Gifts*, a Catholic charismatic newsletter.

Tressa M. Clinger is the mother of three beautiful children. She enjoys writing after the children are in bed for the night and can be reached at sarnjosmom@msn.com

Dawn M. Coder is a 33-year-old mother living in the Tampa Bay area. She has been published in *Personal Journaling* magazine and is currently working on her first novel.

Violet Coetzee is an 85-year-old widow and the mother of four children (two still living), seven grandchildren, and one and a half great-grandchildren. She started writing her memories down a few years ago, at the insistence of her children, to preserve a legacy of a different time and culture for her family. Her submission to *Nudges from God* is the first piece she has submitted for publication.

P. Jeanne Davis is a homemaker and writer living with her husband and two sons. She is a member of NAWW and enjoys attending writer's conferences. She is also studying Spanish and spends her available time traveling in the UK doing family genealogy research. Pat is currently completing her first historical fiction. She can be reached at: Patjeanne@cwcom.net

Rusty Fischer is a full-time freelance writer whose work has appeared everywhere from *Seventeen* magazine to *Chicken Soup for the Preteen Soul*. His latest book, *Beyond the Bookstore: 101 (Other) Places to Sell Your Self-Published Book,* is available at www.Bookbooters.com. He lives and works with his beautiful wife, Martha, in sunny Orlando, Florida.

Johnnie Ann Burgess Gaskill writes a weekly inspirational column for three Georgia newspapers. She is also a feature writer, published poet, and photographer, the author of one book, and a contributing author for others. Her work appears online and in various print publications. www.eThomaston.net/johnnie

Bonnie Compton Hanson, artist/speaker, is the author of several books, including the new *Ponytail Girls* series for girls, plus hundreds of articles, stories, and poems. You can reach her and her lively family—including husband, Don, children, grandchildren, birds, cats, and possums at: 3330 S. Lowell St., Santa Ana, CA 92707   (714)751-7824 email: bonnieh1@worldnet.att.net

Julie Bonn Heath lives in the Pacific Northwest with her family where she is currently at work on a non-ficton book inspired by her adventures in her recent waiting room. You can email her at: juliebonnheath@aol.com

Dorothy Hill, an educator and former foster parent, lives in Potts Camp, Mississippi. When she is not writing, she can be found enjoying her grandchildren (and their parents, of course). She can be reached at: missisip@dixie-net.com

Mark L. Hoffman, an award-winning journalist and reporter, is a freelance writer from picture postcard-like Lancaster County, Pennsylvania. He has been published in a variety of anthologies and in dozens of national magazines, including *Good Housekeeping, Reader's Digest,* and *The Old Farmer's Almanac.* He and his wife Susan reside with their beagle, Mollie, in Lititz. He can be reached at mark@hoffman.org.

Vanessa Bruce Ingold is often referred to as "a walking miracle." Although she's had many more extensive operations since her first hospital departure, she is still very active. She and her husband, Greg, live in Fullerton, California. You may reach her at: JCnessa@aol.com

Karla Jensen is a freelance writer, Lutheran pastor's wife, and mother of three children. Karla has been published by Augsburg Fortress Publishing through the ELCA (church dramas or youth dramas and reader's theatres) and written several children's books she is submitting to publishers. Karla has also authored an audiobook entitled *An Introduction to Co-op Advertising* and is a contributing author in *Forget Me Knots...from the Front Porch.*

Shirley Jump writes romantic comedies for Silhouette Romance. She is the author of *The Virgin's Proposal* (January 2003) and *Close Quarters* (working title)(end of 2003). A 20-year freelance writer, she has also written *How to Publish Your Articles: A Complete Guide to Making the Right Publication Say Yes.*

..aminski resides in Tecumseh, Michigan, with her blended family—her husband, Tom, and children, Sarah and Angela Wyse and Nikki and Tommy Kaminski. Heide is a published author in print and on the Internet. Her Internet site is: http://www.randycuster.net/sandcastles

Kristin Dreyer Kramer was nudged out of advertising agency life and into the life of a wife and freelance writer. A Midwesterner at heart, Kristin now lives in Massachusetts with her new husband, Paul, and is the Editor in Chief of NightsAndWeekends.com. She can be contacted at: krdrkr@hotmail.com

Cathy Laska lives in Wausau, Wisconsin, and aspires to be a freelance writer. Presently, she is working on a book about her missionary journey in Africa. She has also written several inspirational pieces of poetry. Her poem entitled "On Bended Knee" was published in the book *911: The Day America Cried.*

Kelly Ann Malone is a wife, mother to three active boys, and a project analyst in a cancer research department in the health care industry. She has been writing since she was about 12 years old. Published credits include *York University's School of Women's Studies Journal, Cappers Magazine, The Rearview Quarterly, The Penwood Review, The Wesleyan Advocate Magazine,* and many others.

Steven Manchester is the published author of *The Unexpected Storm: The Gulf War Legacy, At The Stroke of Midnight,* and *Jacob Evans.* He has also published several works under the pen name, Steven Herberts. When not spending time with his sons, writing, or promoting his published books/films, this Massachusetts author speaks publicly to troubled children through the "Straight Ahead" Program.

Carole McDonnell is an essayist and fiction writer. Her work is also included in two other anthologies: *Lifenotes: Personal Writings by Black Women* and *Age Ain't Nothin But a Number.* Her scifi novel is called *The Daughters of Men.* http://www.geocities.com/scifiwritir/OreoBlues.html

LaDonna Meredith is a wife and mother, freelance writer, and the former co-owner and Executive Publisher Obadiah Press and *Obadiah Magazine.*

Jennifer Anne F. Messing resides in Oregon with her husband and their three children, is a published author/poet, and is also a licensed hairstylist.

She has a bachelor's degree in Christian Education and a diploma in Freelance Journalism. Her parents, Salvador and Victoria Fabregas, live in Manila, Philippines—Jennifer's birthplace. MnJMessing@cs.com

Tina L. Miller is the author of *When A Woman Prays* and the owner and Editor in Chief of Obadiah Press/*Obadiah Magazine*. She has been published extensively in magazines, newspapers, and trade publications; ghostwritten for individuals and corporations; and edited seven books. Tina lives in Northcentral Wisconsin with her husband, John, and their children, David and Katarina. www.tinalmiller.com tina@tinalmiller.com

Gwen Morrison is a freelance writer and mom of four children, ages six through 17. She has definitely "been there, done that." She claims that her family life alone could keep her in writing material for decades…she is never bored.

Vanessa K. Mullins has completed two novels and is currently working on another. She has written for her local newspaper, several online webzines, and has had numerous pieces accepted and published in both online and print anthologies. *Nudges from God* is the first anthology she has compiled. Email her with your thoughts/comments about the book at: vkmullins@comcast.net

Michael Nabi is president of InTheBible.com, producers of the #1 distributed bible software in the world, Bible Browser. He has done radio programs, produced various Christian music CDs, and several other related projects. Michael also coordinates missions outreaches, i.e. 2002 & 2004 Olympic Games sponsored by many ministries.

Michelle Guthrie Pearson lives with her husband, Jeff, and son, Sean, on their family farm in northern Illinois where she writes and runs her handcrafted soap business. Her work has appeared in numerous publications including *Becoming Family, The Christian Science Monitor,* and the *God Allows U-Turns* series. She is currently working on a children's historical fiction novel. Email: stoneyknoll@lrnet1.com

Helen Kay Polaski is a 17-year newspaper reporter and freelance journalist. Her credits include stories in *Crumbs in the Keyboard, Let Us Not Forget, Vol. I and II, 911: The Day America Cried*, and *Romancing the Soul*, and her own anthology, *Forget Me Knots. . .from the Front Porch.* She is currently working on a second book in the series. Email her at: forgetmeknots@yahoo.com

Avis McGriff Rasmussen is a speaker, accomplished writer, and poet. Her award winning poems include: "Heart & Soul" and "Beneath My Skin I Have A Soul." She has authored numerous inspirational stories. Her latest stories are featured in *More God's Abundance* (Starburst Publishers). She can be reached at P.O. Box 3463, Riverside, CA 92519 or via email: avis_9506@netzero.net

Leigh Platt Rogers was born in Camp Lejeune, North Carolina, and raised all over the world by virtue of her father's occupation (CIA). She is a graduate of the College of William and Mary and is a published writer. She currently resides in Benicia, California, with her husband, Randy.

Vinette Smit was born in February 1964 in the city of Bloemfontein in the Orange Free State in South Africa. Her father was transferred a lot during her childhood, and as a result, "Books were my escape," she says. She still loves books and would like to write a novel one day. She works at a large insurance company and lives in the Eastern suburbs of Pretoria, the Jacaranda City, capital of South Africa.

Nanette Snipes has published articles, columns, and devotions in publications such as *Focus on the Family's LifeWise, The Lookout, Mature Living,* and *Power for Living,* and in compilation books like *Stories for a Teen's Heart, Book 3, Stories for the Spirit-Filled Believer, Chicken Soup for the Christian Family Soul and Christian Woman's Soul.* Contact information: www.nanettesnipes.com and nsnipes@mindspring.com

Pamela Troeppl Kinnaird lives in the Pacific Northwest with her husband and their four children. She is the humor columnist for *The Colorado Daily* and has written for *The Chicago Tribune, The Milwaukee Journal Sentinel,* and *The Seattle Post Intelligencer.* She is a member of The Church of Jesus Christ of Latter-day Saints. You can reach her at pamela_troeppl@yahoo.com

Shelley Ann Wake is a writer and poet based in Australia. She lives in a small country town with her husband and spends her days writing articles, stories, essays, and poetry. Her work has been published in various anthologies, magazines, and ezines. Email: mish_writer@hotmail.com

L. Pat Williams is a reporter/editor and has worked as a reporter/ copyeditor for *LifeTimes* publication; as a freelance writer for *SCREEN* Magazine, *Metro Commuter,* and *StreetWise* newspaper; as a proofreader/

feature writer for *Chicago Defender* (all located in Chicago, Illinois); and as Chicago stringer for *Renaissance Women's* e-zine.

Darlene Zagata is a freelance writer and poet. Her work has appeared in several publications, both electronic and print. She is a mother of four children and two grandchildren. Besides writing, Darlene enjoys reading and researching the paranormal. She views life as the ultimate inspiration and hopes to someday write something that will continue to uplift and inspire others beyond her lifetime.

Permissions:

~~OBADIAH MAGAZINE~~

For People Who Live Their Lives to Love and Serve the Lord

Just $15 for 4 quarterly issues!

Canadian subscriptions: $18
Other International subscriptions: $20

Subscribe Me!

Mail To: Obadiah Magazine
c/o Obadiah Press
607 N. Cleveland Street
Merrill, WI 54452

Name: _____

Address: _____

_____

City, State, Zip: _____

Country: _____Phone: _____

Include check or money order (US funds) for each subscription ordered.

Initial Subscription: _____ Renewal: _____ (check one)

Send a Gift Subscription:

Mail To: Obadiah Magazine
c/o Obadiah Press
607 N. Cleveland Street
Merrill, WI 54452

Please send a gift subscription TO:

Name: _____

Address: _____

_____

City, State, Zip: _____

Country: _____Phone: _____

FROM: _____

NOTE TO INCLUDE WITH FIRST ISSUE: _____

_____

_____

Include check or money order (US funds) for each subscription ordered.

This form may be freely reproduced.

Order Other Books Published by:

OBADIAH PRESS

Qty. Ordered

___**Running As Fast As I Can@** $16.95

by Lois Hilton Spoon

Exactly one year from the day she was told she would die from terminal cancer, Lois ran a ten mile race! A story of hope, God's miraculous intervention, and life.

___**Good Mourning, Lord@** $15.95

by Alyice Edrich

When her child died, a part of Alyice did, too. Raw and emotionally poignant, she shares her feelings and provides room for you to journal your own feelings as you work through *your* grief, knowing there is no "right way" to grieve.

___**When A Woman Prays@** $15.95

by Tina L. Miller

Miracles can happen when a woman prays...Tap into the power of prayer and change your life. Develop your own very personal, intimate relationship with God.

___**911, The Day America Cried@** $15.95

Compiled by Victoria Walker

A collection of poems, letters, and stories on an American tragedy. Written by 80+ authors from across the U.S. and Canada

___**Nudges from God@** $15.95

Compiled by Vanessa K. Mullins

An anthology of inspiration. A collection of stories that will touch your heart and soul.

___**Forget Me Knots...from the Front Porch@** $15.95

Compiled by Helen Kay Polaski

An anthology of heartfelt stories from around the world.

Total for books ordered above = $_____

___# of books ordered x $2 S/H per book = $_____

TOTAL = $_____

VISA
MasterCard

☐ My check or money order is enclosed. **OR**

☐ Please charge my Mastercard or VISA

My credit card number is: _____

It expires on: _____ My name exactly as shown
on my credit card is: _____

Mail your order to:

Obadiah Press
607 N. Cleveland St.
Merrill, WI 54452

Fax: 715-536-3167

_____ _____
Signature   Date

Or Call
Toll Free:
1-866-536-3167

Ship Books to:

Name_____

Address_____

_____

(If credit card order and address is different than the address to which credit card statements are sent, please also include credit card mailing address.)

Prices shown are US funds. Include $2 additional for Canadian orders and $4 additional for other international orders. Quantity discounts available. Write for information. This form may be freely reproduced.

OBADIAH PRESS

A Christian Publishing House

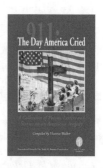

| *Good Mourning, Lord* by Alyice Edrich ISBN 0-9713266-4-9 $15.95 U.S. | *Forget Me Knots... from the Front Porch* compiled by Helen Kay Polaski ISBN 0-9713266-8-1 288 pages, $15.95 U.S. | *911: The Day America Cried* compiled by Victoria Walker ISBN 0-9713266-5-7 288 pages, $15.95 U.S. |

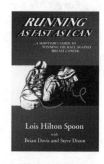

| *When A Woman Prays* by Tina L. Miller ISBN 0-9713266-1-4 176 pages, $15.95 U.S. | *Nudges from God* compiled by Vanessa K. Mullins ISBN 0-9713266-7-3 288 pages, $15.95 U.S. | *Running As Fast As I Can* by Lois Hilton Spoon ISBN 0-9713266-0-6 168 pages, $16.95 U.S. |

Use the form on the reverse (or a photocopy of the form) to order any of Obadiah's books directly from the publisher.
Or, ask for them at your local bookstore.